To Maureen and Don

Love and good wis

Gloria Sept.

AN EASEL IN THE FAMILY

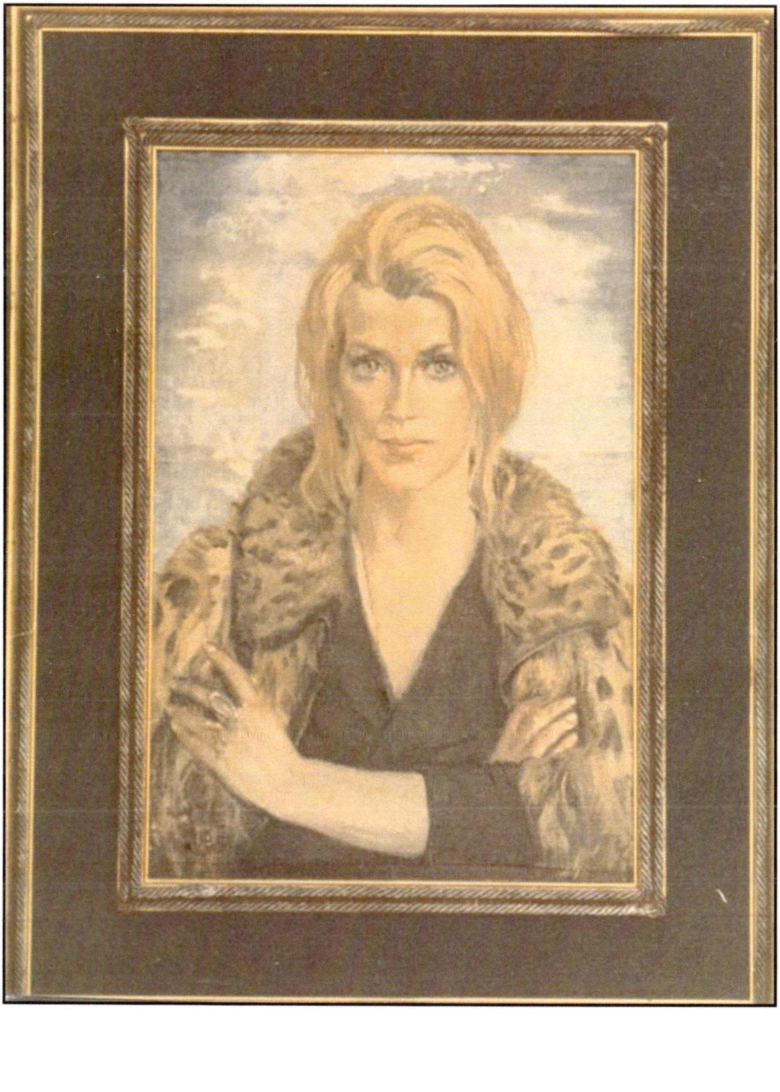

GLORIA JARVIS SMITH

An Easel in the Family

First published in 2005

Published by Gloria Jarvis Smith,
38 St Radigund's Street, Canterbury, Kent CT1 2AA

ISBN 0-9543656-2-3

Printed by Oyster Press, Chestfield, Whitstable, Kent

Acknowledgements

I should like to express how much I owe to the following artists whom I had the privilege of studying under at St Martin's:

Robin Guthrie, whose wonderful exhibition of drawings in ink and watercolour at Colnaghi's, Bond Street in the late 1940s burst upon my conscience as a revelation and inspiration.

James Bateman R.A., who had the knack of bringing out the individuality of a student, whether in drawing, painting or composition – of which he was an ace.

Barry Craig, painter, who kept up one's confidence by always finding in the work he was criticising some saving grace.

To Piers Plowright, now retired, radio producer at the BBC, thank you for your encouragement in my writing.

My parents, too, have my heartfelt thanks in accepting those nine years of study.

The Society of Women Writers and Journalists for allowing me to reproduce from The Woman Journalist Margaret Crosland's Profile of me, with special thanks to her.

Thanks are due to the journal, L'Eventail for their article about me in their section: Abroad in Belgium.

Introduction

Few infants succeed in pronouncing my name, Gloria – least of all myself as a tot. After the ritual of climbing into my parents' bed of a morning and squeezing myself between them, I would grasp their necks in a joint hug and breathe a contented: "Mummy, Daddy, Goya!" By unwittingly turning my name into that of the Spanish painter, Goya, I had foretold the future. Little did I know his inspiration would loom large in the artistic career Fate had mapped out for me, when the greater part of my life would be dominated by the easel - symbol of so many of my painting endeavours.

Contents

Cover: Same model, same pose, drawn from different angles.

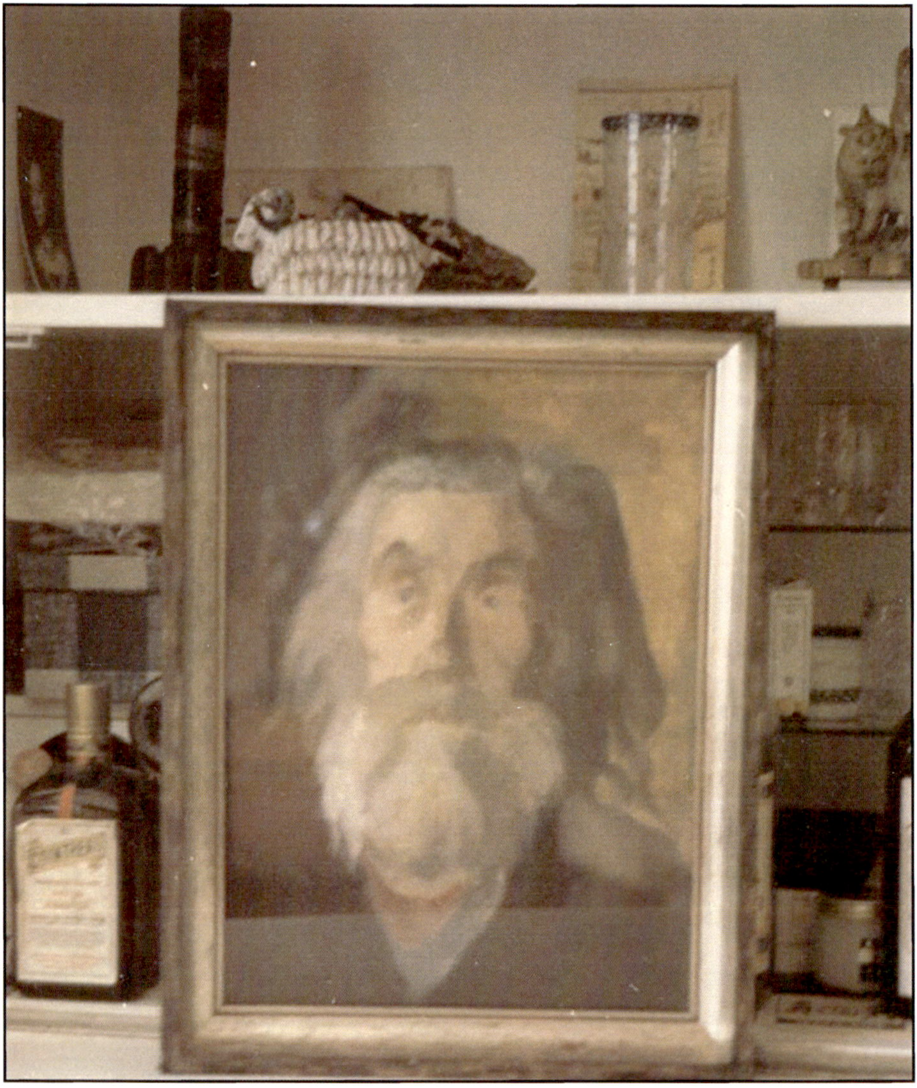

A corner of the artist's studio

Trunks and Flapping Ears

"She has the distinction of having drawn Quentin Crisp in the nude" was how a friend introduced me at her recent house-warming. Naturally the announcement acted as a magnet on my fellow partygoers, who gathered round to know more.

But the artistic world frequented in my youth belongs to those student days yet to come in this book.

To start with one's own dawn – that awesome thing called birth – mine occurred on St. Patrick's Day (a reason for nursing a soft spot for the Irish when their patron saint's day comes round). By choosing the 17th, Fate did "beware the Ides of March" (I was luckier than Shakespeare's Julius Caesar).

My sketches of Quentin Crisp are ahead of that infant stage when suffice it to grasp a pencil and any scrap of paper to hand, and discover the wondrous feat of drawing on a flat surface something recognisable – and living – in my case, an elephant. So loveable a creature I rode at the zoo became my forte. With their trunks and big flapping ears repeated over and over again, it set me on the artistic trail which, from then on, I seemed to take for granted.

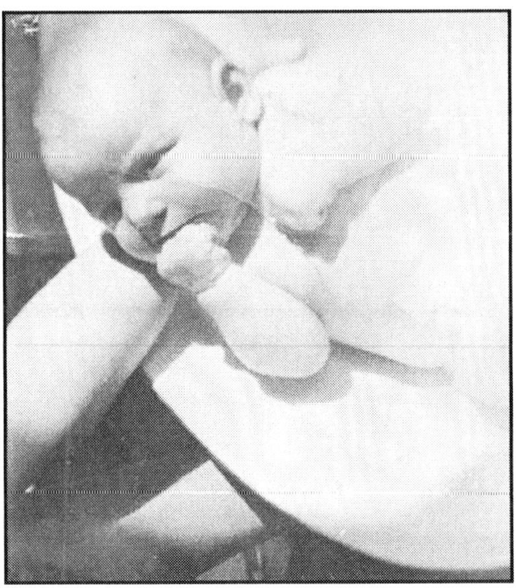

Gloria Patricia Jarvis
Aged 3 months

The impulse came from seeing my father draw – a daily occurrence in our household when he did freelance work on the side. Early marriage had halted his training in architecture, a discipline, however, that gave him an advantage in his job as an advertising artist. What was then Commercial Art has today been revamped with a posher ring as Graphic Art. On many an evening or weekend he would be at his easel drawing in detail examples of one of the stylish motor cars of the early 1930s, the Studebaker, commissioned from Dad by its promoter in Britain, Captain Fitzmaurice. This beautiful auto/beast in the de luxe class afforded my father enough private work to augment his income.

Babyhood was full of discoveries anew. But it was the experience at first hand of the fragility of eggs that lingers as my first recollection.

Picture one of those high prams of the 1920s, and in it a baby parked outside a shop my mother had popped into for a second, leaving me with a bag of eggs amongst the shopping to whet my curiosity – which turned to wonder when, leaning over the side, I watched 6 eggs plop, plop, one after the other, and turn into a row of yellow yolks on the pavement.

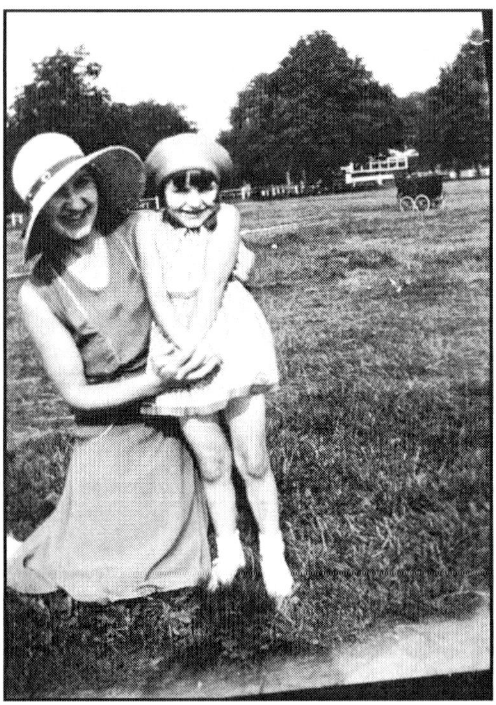

My returning young mother's burst of laughter was yet another surprise for this tot with the questioning gaze, all innocence in her pram – and magnificent vehicles they were, too, in those days, built high to keep the little dears above the dust of the highway.
A shiny black pair of wellington boots I was taken to buy at a shoe shop in College Road, Harrow (the town where we lived) made its mark on the memory. "Please, God, make it rain tomorrow" was my nightly prayer – which when answered turned me into an ecstatic Christopher Robin splashing about in puddles.

Having grown up in John Betjeman's Metroland, I find in recent years his poem "Harrow-on-the-Hill" so very evocative. In my teens the historic site was the focus for a walk, and I, too, when mounting the hill had the feeling that over the brow lay the sea and that the churchyard was full of sailors' graves.

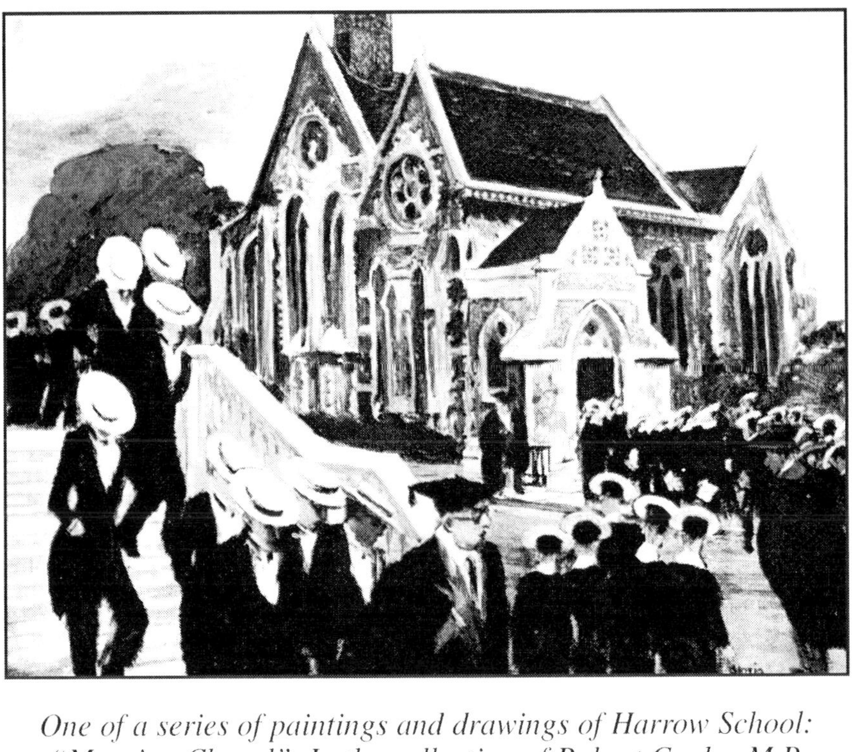

One of a series of paintings and drawings of Harrow School: "Morning Chapel". In the collection of Robert Cooke, M.P.

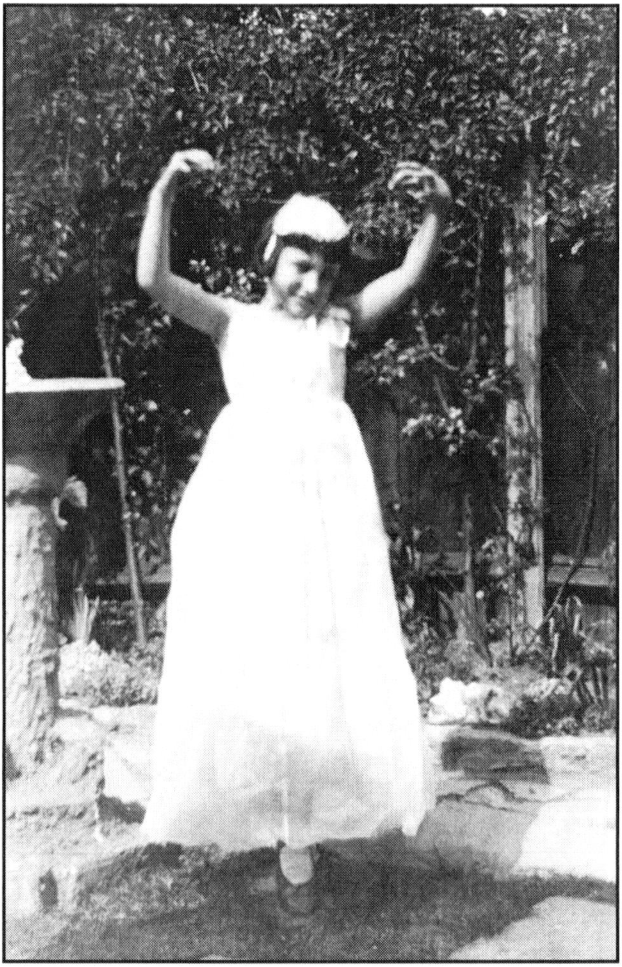

Rehearsing for a ballet display

Memory holds the key to so much else besides: the street cries of my infancy – as once again the rag and bone man, with cart and raucous holler, walks swiftly down our street; the muffin man swinging his bell around tea-time and balancing the tray of muffins on his head (and they were proper muffins: flat, light and round, eaten toasted and buttered). In Piccadilly Circus, skirting Eros, the flower ladies with their baskets of blooms and posies in outstretched hands, cooing, "Lovely sweet violets, gents - lovely roses." Occasionally a man, elegantly dressed for an evening out, would lean from a taxi to buy flowers for his lady-love. The ritual of the lamplighter progressing down our road at dusk – what better than his nightly task to round off all those yester-years of childhood.

My formative years I have already dealt with in my two published histories of my family, "A Jarvis Tapestry" (parts l and ll) from Tudor to recent times, with many drawings of my inimitable grandfather who figured so much in my young life.

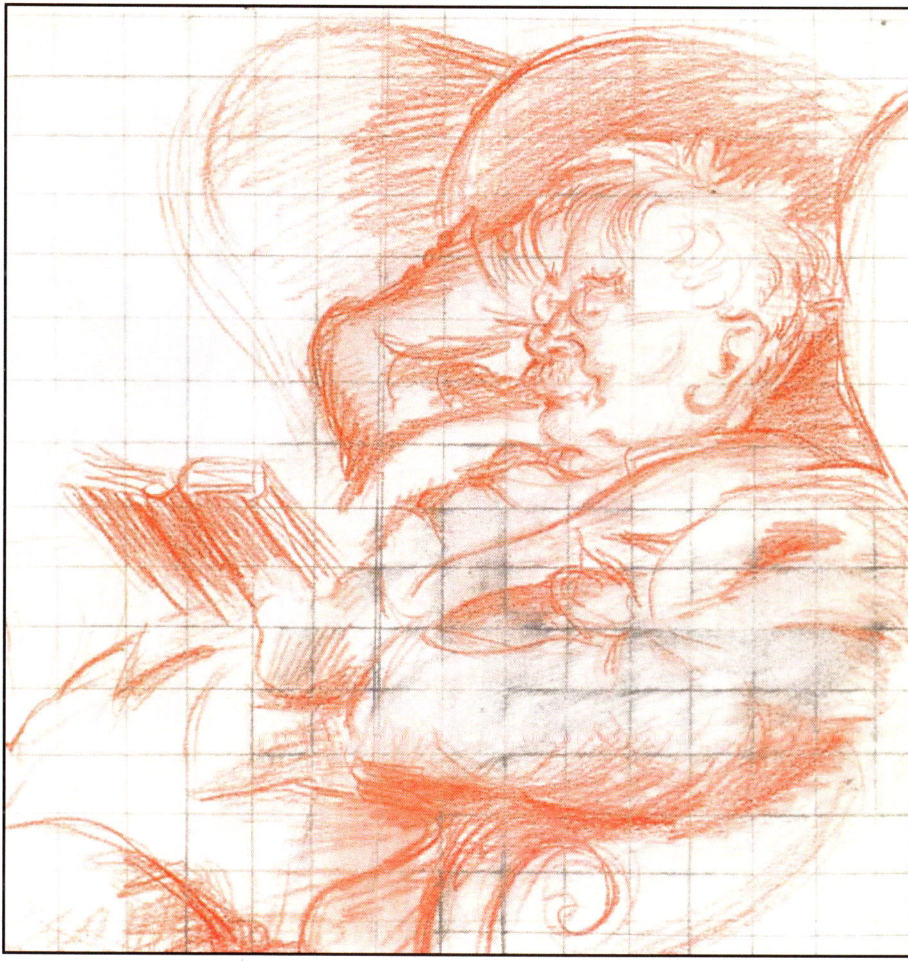

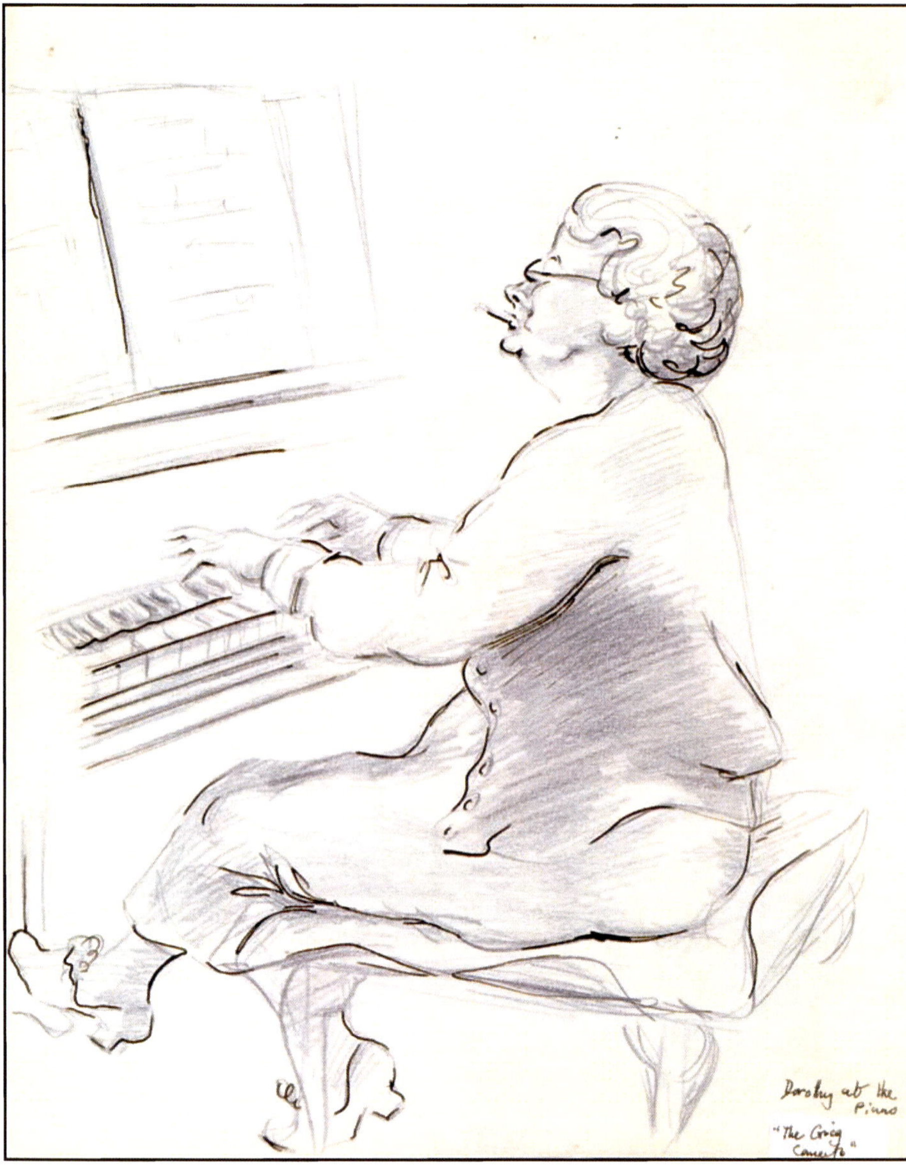

Auntie Dorothy at the Piano

TO WRITE, PERCHANCE TO DRAW...

The Second World War was not quite over - but schooldays were. It was time to decide upon a career. Writing and art were my best subjects. Designing for the stage seems like a day-dream in retrospect, but as a romantic schoolgirl I hankered after creating such exotic designs as Léon Bakst's for the Russian ballets.

I enrolled for a course on Stage Design at St Martin's School of Art in Charing Cross Road – the die was cast.

It took place in the Dress Department under its head, Muriel Pemberton, who, at the moment I entered, was supervising the finishing touches to an enormous piece of camouflage for the war effort – a huge net appliquéd with rag-like materials simulating leaves, destined to conceal some military feature in the British Isles.

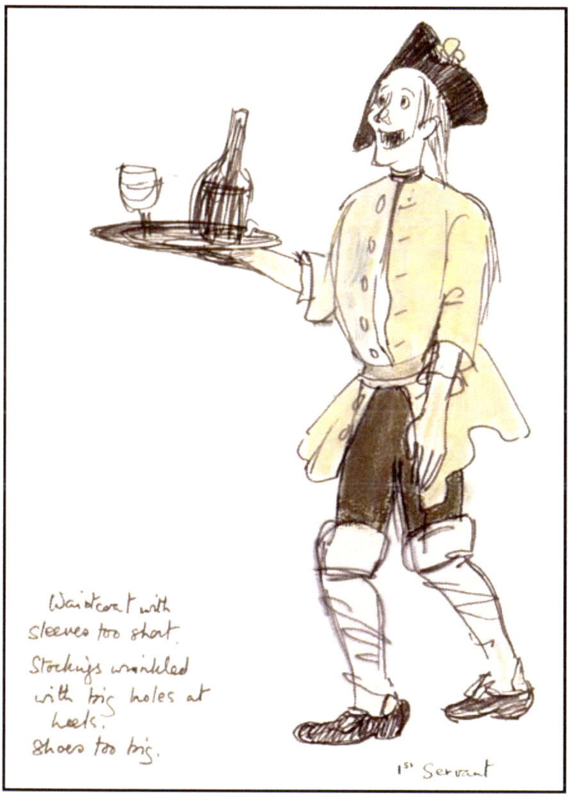

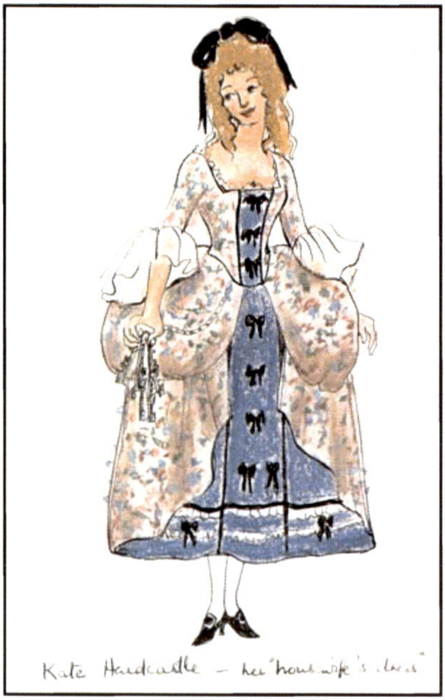

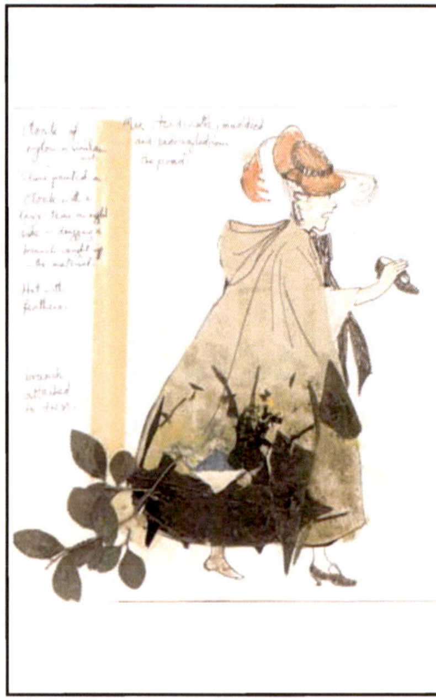

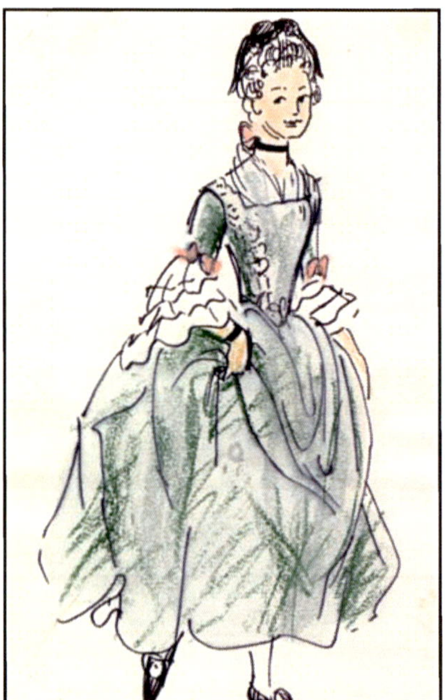

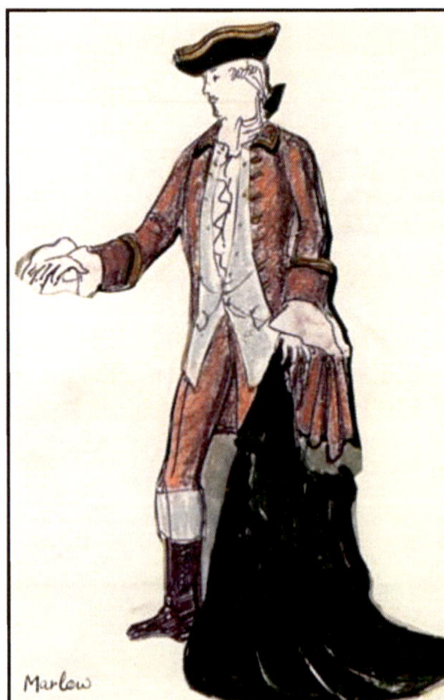

A few of my designs for "She Stoops to Conquer"

Miss Pemberton was an inspiring tutor especially in building up a student's confidence. The programme consisted of the histories of costume and furniture; dress and set designs for specific plays – and life drawing (which tested the ability of the student).

During three enjoyable years in which I assisted the costume designer on a film at Denham studios one holiday, I came to realise that there was little drawing involved – it was mainly pattern cutting, sewing on buttons and making accessories – such as muffs and toning down the brightness of the buttons of the Pearly Kings and Queens (in the film I was on: "London Town").

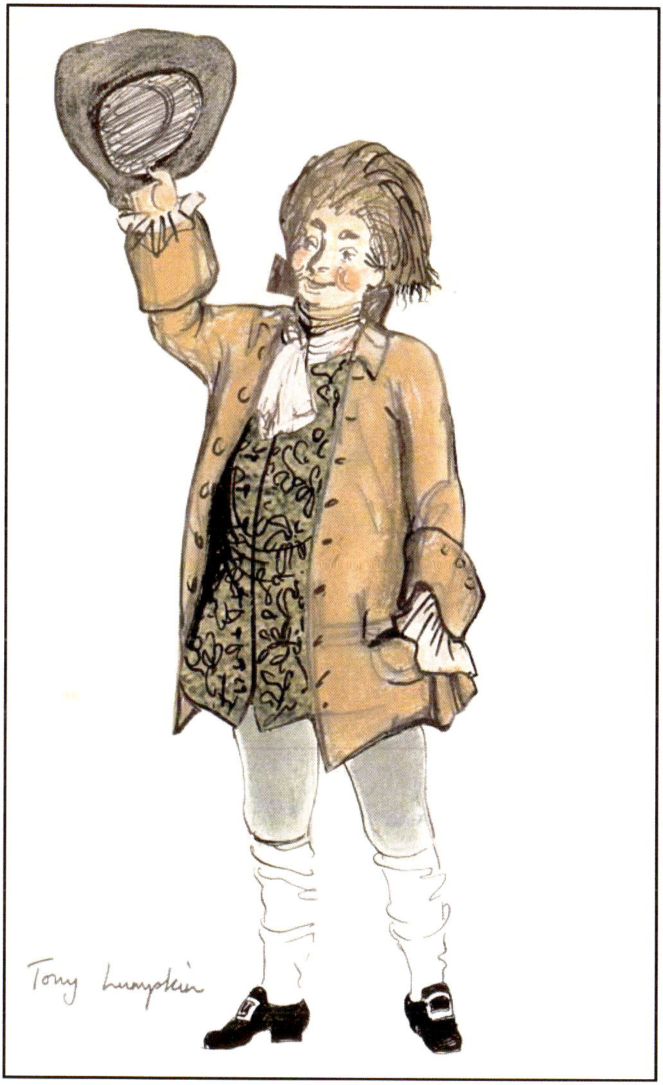

Designing sets for films had a similar drawback in that it was not enough to have ideas expressed in a first rate drawing. You had to have a grounding in architecture and engineering to know how the set should be built – I wasn't that way minded. Said art director John Bryan: "I only know of one woman art director – Carmen Dillon." Having seen at first hand the true nature of the jobs I had wanted to pursue brought me down to earth, and the realisation that a more practical way of earning a living would be in teaching. I switched to the course that would qualify me: The National Diploma in Painting and Design (Ministry of Education). Besides, my ambition now was to paint.

It meant another three years at St Martin's but my understanding parents agreed; and a scholarship awarded by the London County Council helped.

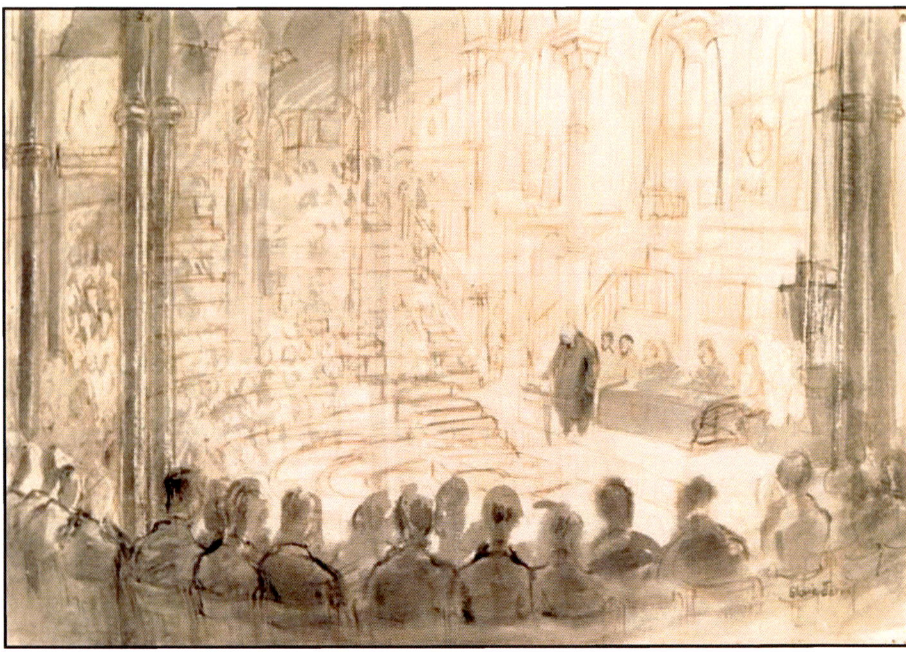

November, 1950. Sketch from life for my oil painting of Churchill's last visit but one to Harrow School to hear the boys sing the school songs.
These annual visits in November began during the war and which he regarded as nostalgic occasions. That year another verse had been added to "Forty Years On" It was "Sixty Years On", written in his honour. I had been given permission to sit and sketch high up at the back.

(62) [1950

GALLERY No. IX.

DRAWINGS, ENGRAVINGS AND ETCHINGS.
(Nos. 1038-1188).

1038 Preliminary design for "The Meat Market"—water colour and charcoal .. .. *Gloria P. Jarvis*

1039 Seated Nude—chalk .. .. *Frank Dobson*, A.

1040 The late Sid Field—sanguine and black chalk .. .. *Dame Laura Knight*, R.A.

1041 Barcombe Mills, Sussex—chalk and wash.. .. .. *E. A. Sallis Benney*

1042 Public Bar—pen and wash .. *James T. Robinson*

1043 Nude Study—chalk .. .. *Frank Dobson*, A.

1044 Study of an Old Man—pen and wash *Christopher J. Alexander*

1045 Mr. Brazier—pencil and chalk .. *Adrian G. Beach*

1046 Sam Golding, Cobbler—pen and wash *Joseph M. T. Acheson*

1047 An Austrian Woman—wash .. .. *Hugh A. Finney*

1048 Fragments of a Demolished World—pen and chalk.. .. .. *Brian Bradshaw*

1049 The Flute Player—sanguine *Charles Wheeler*, R.A.

No. 353

ROYAL ACADEMY OF ARTS

THE ONE HUNDRED AND EIGHTY-SECOND EXHIBITION
1950.

EXHIBITOR'S VARNISHING & SEASON TICKET

ADMIT THE BEARER

On NON-MEMBERS' VARNISHING DAY, Monday, April 24, from 9 a.m. to 7 p.m.

To THE PRIVATE VIEW, Friday, April 28, from 10 a.m. to 7 p.m.

AND TO THE EXHIBITION AT ANY TIME WHEN IT IS OPEN TO THE PUBLIC (Weekdays, 9.30 a.m. to 7 p.m.; Sundays, 2 to 6 p.m. April 29—Aug. 7.)

Signature of Exhibitor } Gloria P. Jarvis.

This Ticket must be signed by the Exhibitor, who must also sign his or her name in the book at the turnstile each time on entering the Exhibition. It can only be used by the person whose name is signed on it, and if presented by anyone else will be cancelled and not renewed.

N.B.—There will be no admittance without the production of this Ticket, which cannot be renewed if lost or destroyed.

W. R. M. LAMB, *Secretary.*

NOT TRANSFERABLE.

[P.T.O.

Events come crowding back from that end of the war period. The Chelsea Arts Ball was a bohemian send-off to the New Year. Mounted at the Albert Hall by the Chelsea Arts Club, whose members were most of the distinguished artists of the day, its climax of the evening consisted of floats, each with a tableau designed by one of the London art schools. Every ball-goer was in fancy dress, striking a carnival atmosphere. When the speeches of the first Royal Academy of Arts dinner after the war were broadcast by the BBC the one made by its President, Sir Alfred Munnings, caused a furore. Ever robust in his language, his expletives were directed against modern art, then coming to the fore. Suddenly he turned to Churchill (honorary Royal Academician) and said:

"If we saw Picasso walking towards us we would give him a kick up the backside!"

(ensuring the end of such future broadcasts!)

I believe it was 1948; two years later I sent in a drawing to the Royal Academy Summer Exhibition - a figurative composition entitled "The Smithfield Meat Market"; the central porter, stopping in his tracks with a quarter of beef, poses with a grin reminiscent of Fernandel, comic French actor.

What an exciting experience to send in for the first time, picture under arm, while hurrying along the approach to the side entrance of Burlington House to hand it in; stacked onto a trolley, it would be carted away into the bowels of the Academy to eventually pass before the voting committee of Royal Academicians. Weeks later the blue sending in card came back, announcing your fate. If lucky, you hoped to find your work hung "on the line" yet grateful if above, dubbed "skyed", I was delighted to see my "Smithfield" there at all – and quite in awe when after the private view I received an invitation to be listed in "Who's Who in Art".

An up to date enclosure in the latest edition of "Who's Who in Art":

JARVIS, Gloria, N.D.D.; Médaille d'Argent Paris (1976); artist in oil, water-colour, pastel, ink, gouache; lecturer on historic costume and instructor in costume drawing, Polytechnic, Regent St. (1950-63); s/d of: Daughter of R. V. Jarvis, artist m: Raymond Smith, B.A (1964). Educ: Heathfield School, Harrow; Aylesbury Grammar School; Studied: St. Martin's School of Art, London, under James Bateman, R.A., the history of art at Florence University. Exhib: R.A., N.E.A.C., Leicester Galleries; one-man shows Brussels (1970..). Work in collections: Abbot Hall A.G., Kendal; Museum of the Dynasty, Brussels; International Museum of Carnival and Mask, Binche, Belgium; and private collections. Commissions: numerous portraits and genre paintings, Brussels Publications: work repro.: Macmillan, Brussels Times. Short stories broadcast by B.B.C.; biography. Clubs: Soc. of Women Writers and Journalists. Signs work:

"Gloria Jarvis." Address: 38 St Radigunds Street, Canterbury Kent CT1 2AA

En Route to the Grubdump: Hermaphrodites al Fresco

London was a life class in itself. On our way to art school of a morning some of us innocents straight from the suburbs were not daring enough to risk being seen going up close to the intriguing windows of the sex shops down Charing Cross Road to satisfy our curiosity.

Forces on leave were everywhere. Free French and Belgian, Dutch and Polish, among others who had got away in time, dotted the art schools. In the streets and parks American doughboys could be a menace – even sitting on the pavement outside their forces' club down Shaftesbury Avenue, tempting female passersby with offers of silk stockings and chocolate; on rare occasions nylons were the bait.

The Astoria at the top of Charing Cross Road, a cinema converted into a ballroom, put on a daily matineé. Many a student would play truant from class to boogie-woogie with the forces crowding the dance floor.

All the passages and alleys leading off Charing Cross Road suggested Hogarth territory, and, in particular, the one opposite St. Martin's School of Art on its way to reach St Giles Churchyard; you felt that Beer Street and Gin Lane could not be far away. That was the route to the Grubdump – so-called by students who took advantage of its cheap lunches subsidised by London County Council. On scrubbed tables in rough and ready décor, the basic fare offered gave value for a mere shilling – or was it sixpence? So very long ago now.

The most memorable feature of this passage was the bombed house, two of its outside brick walls in semi-ruins. We clambered over the rubble and peered into a room open like a proscenium and displaying a frescoed ceiling. Several hermaphrodites, fast fading because of exposure to the elements since the blitz, floated across a patchy bluish sky.

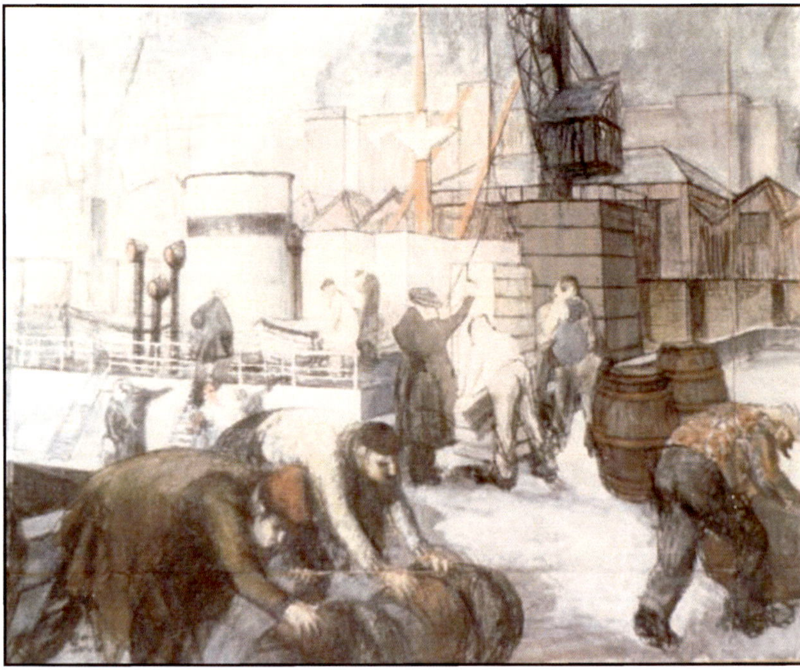

Unloading the Sherry, 1950, at St Katherine's Dock, London. Commissioned to hang in the offices of Royal Decree Sherry (Jarvis and Halliday) in St James's.

The sketch (for the larger oil painting was done from many sketches made at the dock). On my arrival the second day at the dock, I overheard one of the dockers shout: "Rembrandt's here!" (typical of the waggish remarks they could make).

Since acquired by the Museum of Docklands, London.

Thumbs Down for Dress Design

Switching from my original theatrical design course to that of the Diploma in Drawing and Design (preliminary to the Diploma in Painting), I was advised to take my craft subject in dress design (which had an affinity with stage design).

Dior's New Look had burst on the fashion scene, with its spectacular contrast to war-time austerity; it was excitingly theatrical so I worked at my craft like one inspired. But this did not excite me enough to plan a career in fashion; and although in the exam result I came top in the country, this did not tempt me to go on and take the successive Diploma in Dress Design, for my ardent desire was to take it in Painting.

My Professor of Composition was the Royal Academician, James Bateman – Jimmy to his friends. He was enthusiastic about my figurative sketches – and had thwarted the authorities in their attempts to coerce me into taking the Diploma in Dress Design. "They're just thinking of results for the school!" he said. In so doing he had stuck his neck out – and earned my undying gratitude.

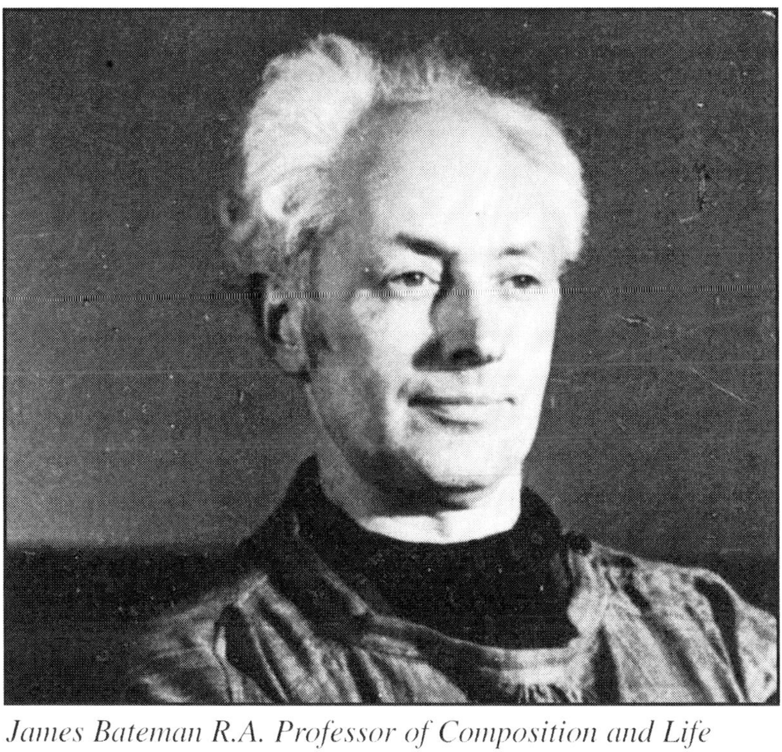

James Bateman R.A. Professor of Composition and Life drawing at St Martin's School of Art in the late 1940s and the 1950s

JAMES BATEMAN, R.A., A.R.W.S.
~~25A GLEBE PLACE~~, CHELSEA, S.W.3.
TEL. FLA. 1972 (HOME) PRO. 1760

No 3 Chelsea Manor Studios
Flood St.

June 14th/50

To whom it may concern.

I have real pleasure in writing on behalf of Miss Gloria Jarvis. She has been one of a group of about 30 students attending my Composition class for the Diploma Students at St Martins School of Art. I look upon her as the most gifted & hard working of them all. Her work may not have an immediate appeal, but in my opinion it possesses rare personal qualities and is full of character.

I can highly recommend her for a post as teacher of this subject & others in which she is qualified.

J Bateman.

Later on, he asked me to assist him on his commission to paint the Whitbread calendar, in which my knowledge of costume would be useful for the subject: the fairs of Britain, some of which were historical.

I joined his Post Diploma course in 1950 at St Martin's School of Art. James Bateman gave invaluable advice in sketching people in movement (in public places) if we were making studies for a composition. The aim was to express the maximum with the minimum of means, by taking advantage of the use of different media. We learned to capture the essence of a pose, which was all we had time for in the 5, 10 and 15 minutes allotted us.

Even the models caught the spirit of improvisation and joined in the fun. We collected props to dress up a model and strike a mood. A top hat, a bottle of "absinthe" could conjure up a Toulouse Laurtrec character; or, if female, the model might press her whole weight on an old fashioned iron to evoke a Degas.

If a model failed to turn up Bateman would go down into the Charing Cross Road and bring back a more interesting substitute from among the passers-by. There were plenty of down and outs ready to earn a few bob.

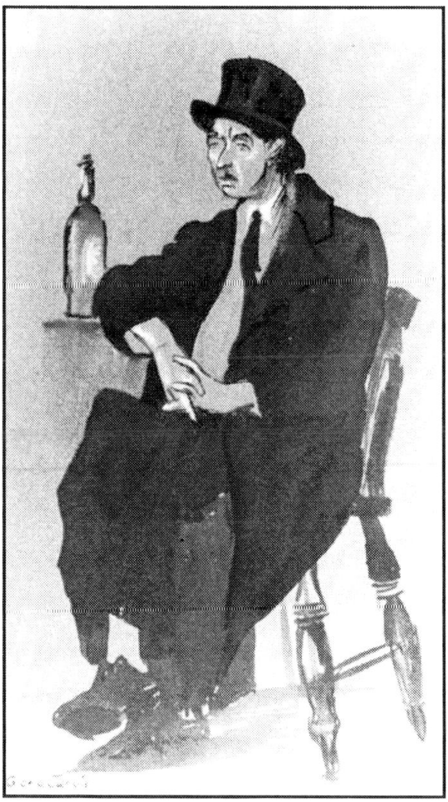

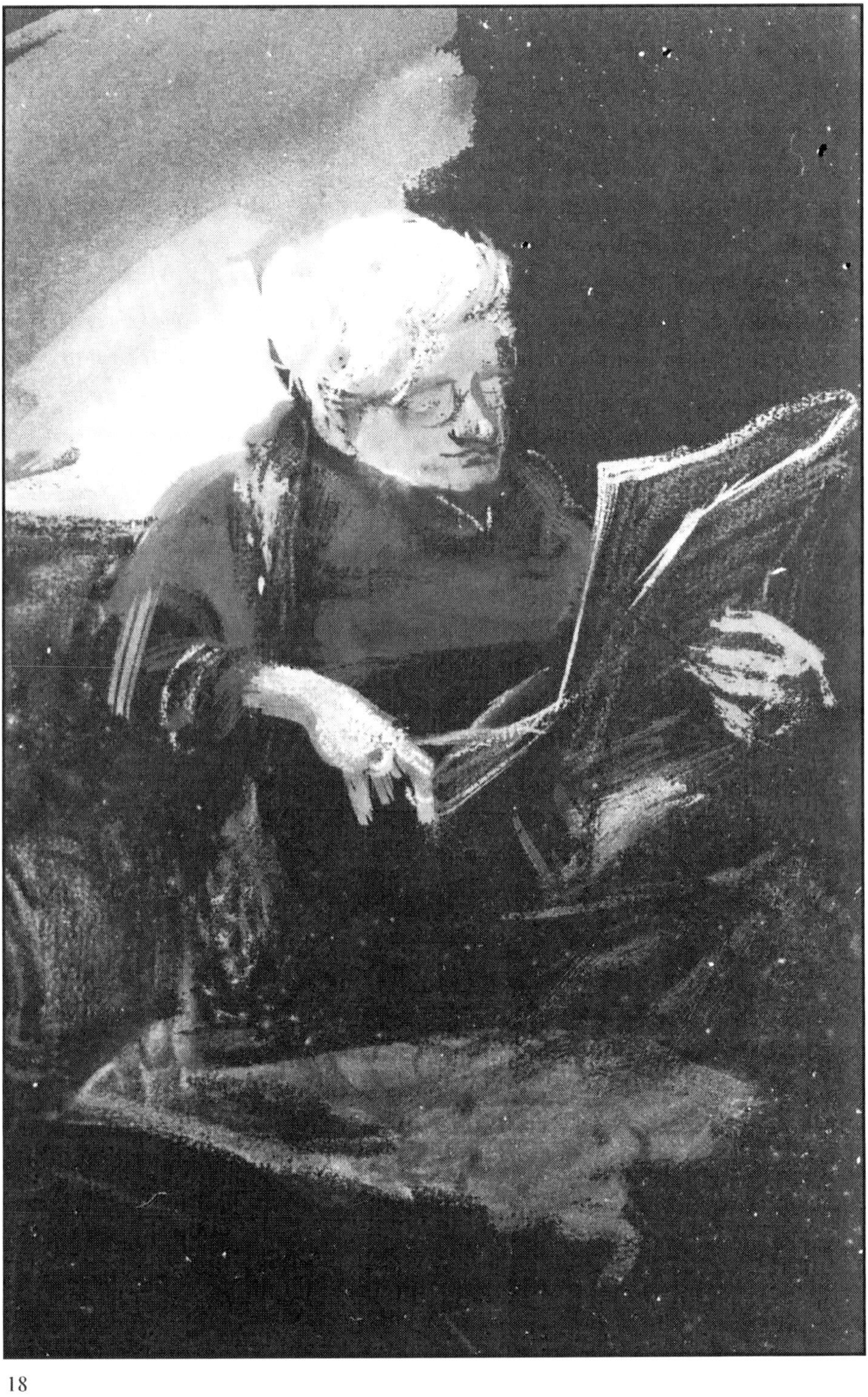

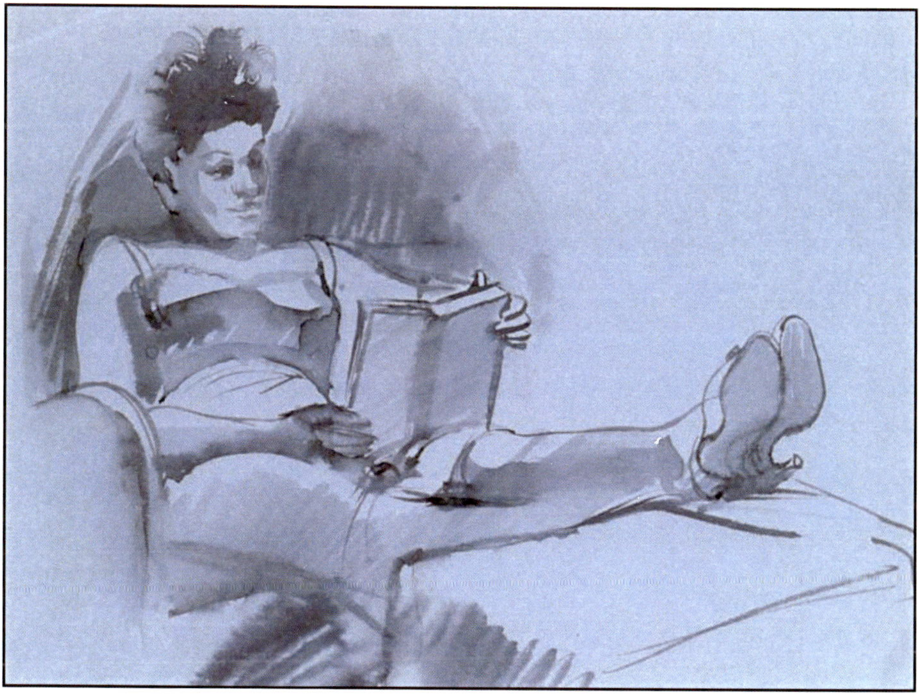

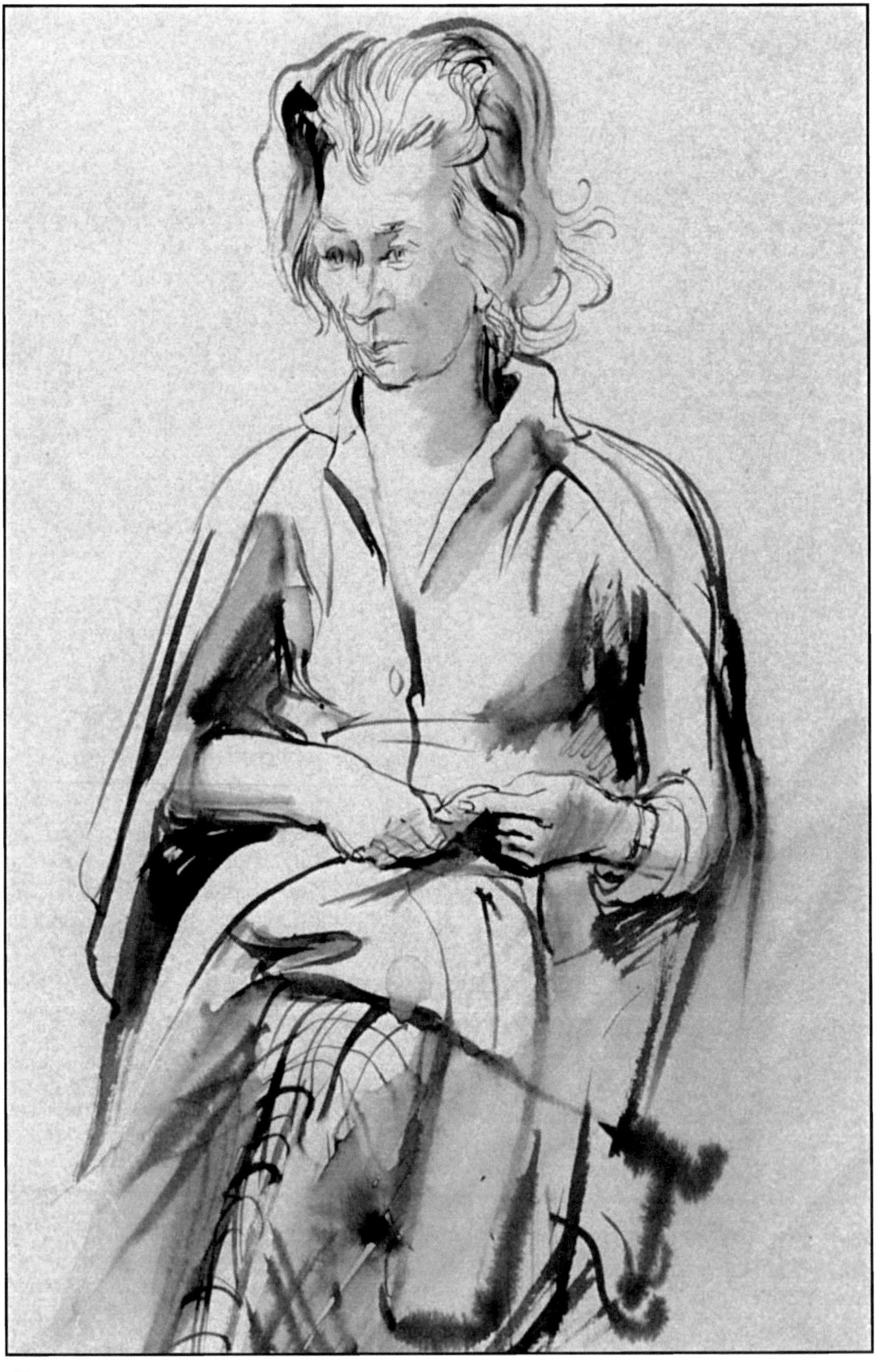

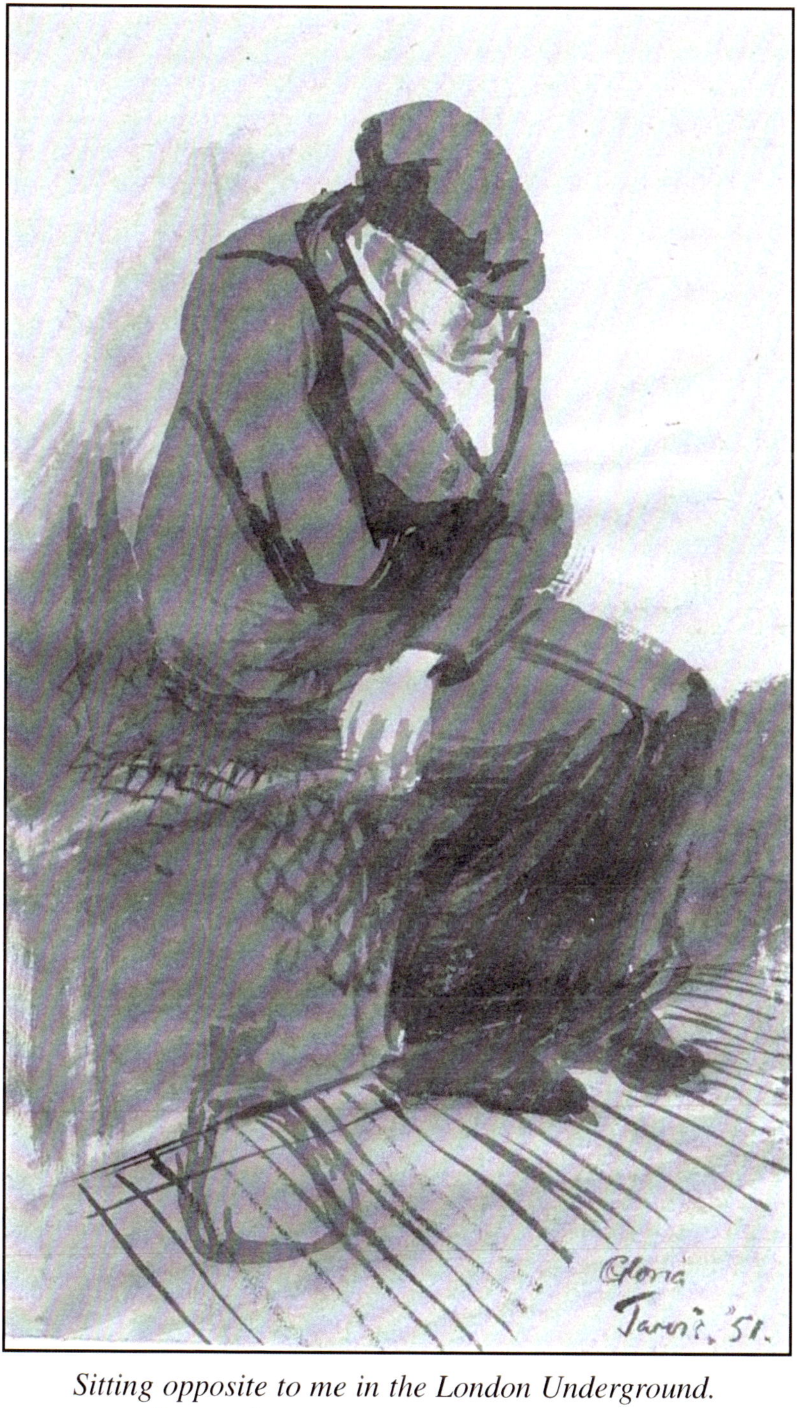

Sitting opposite to me in the London Underground.
Drawn from memory when I got home.

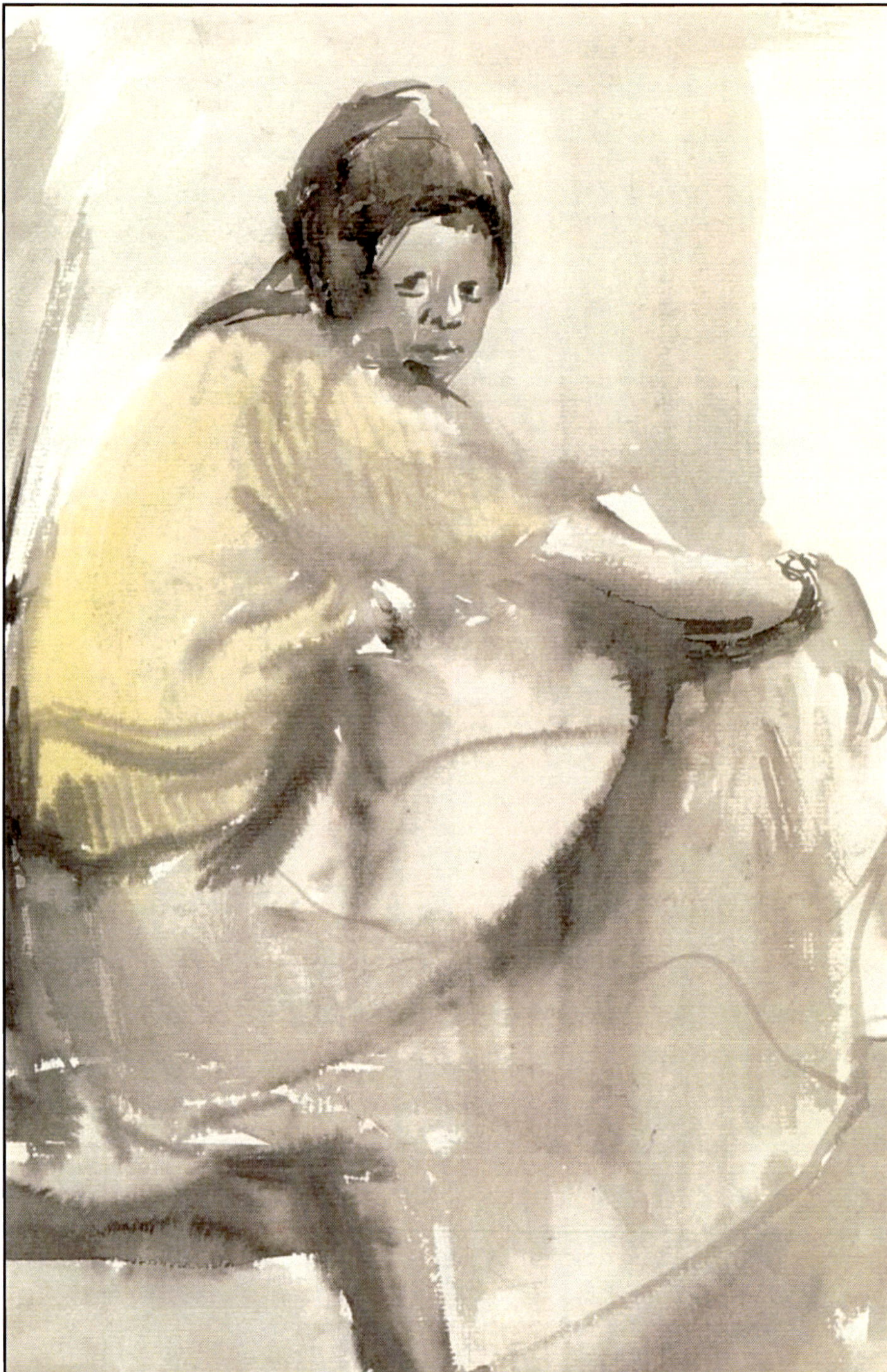

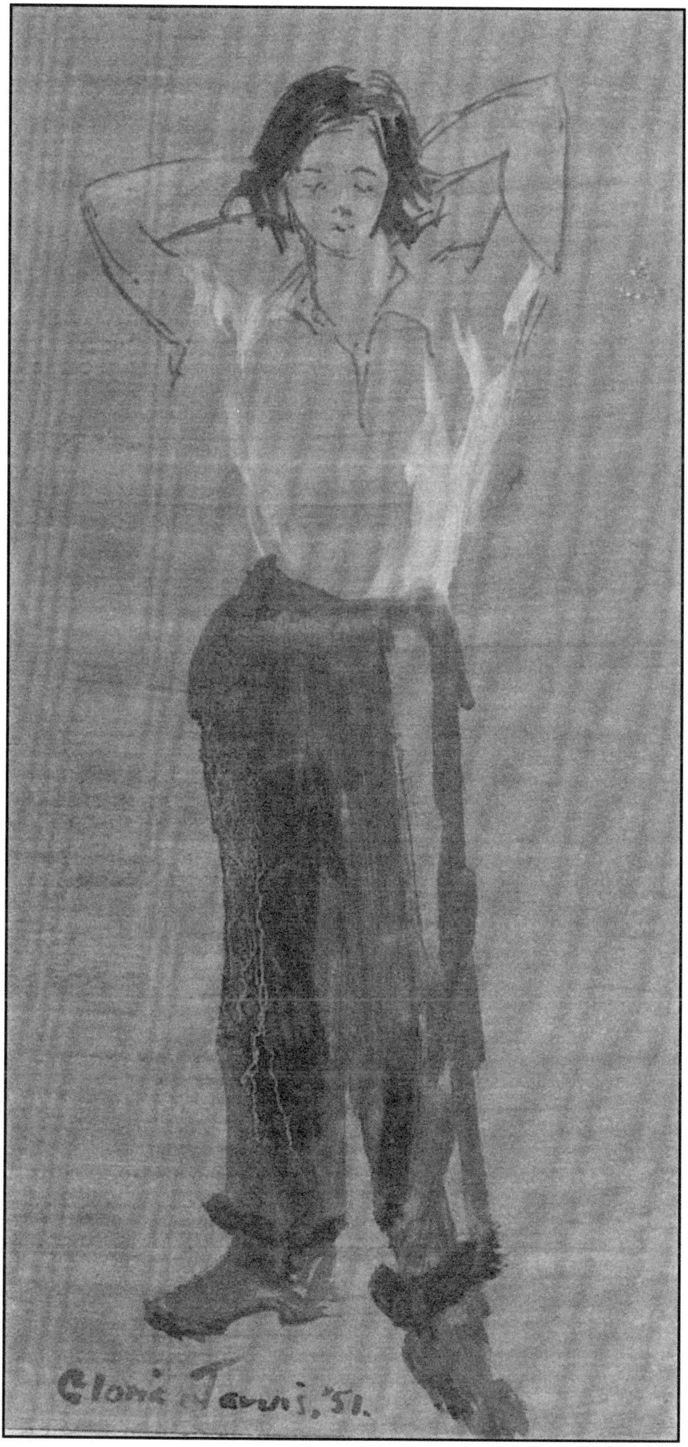

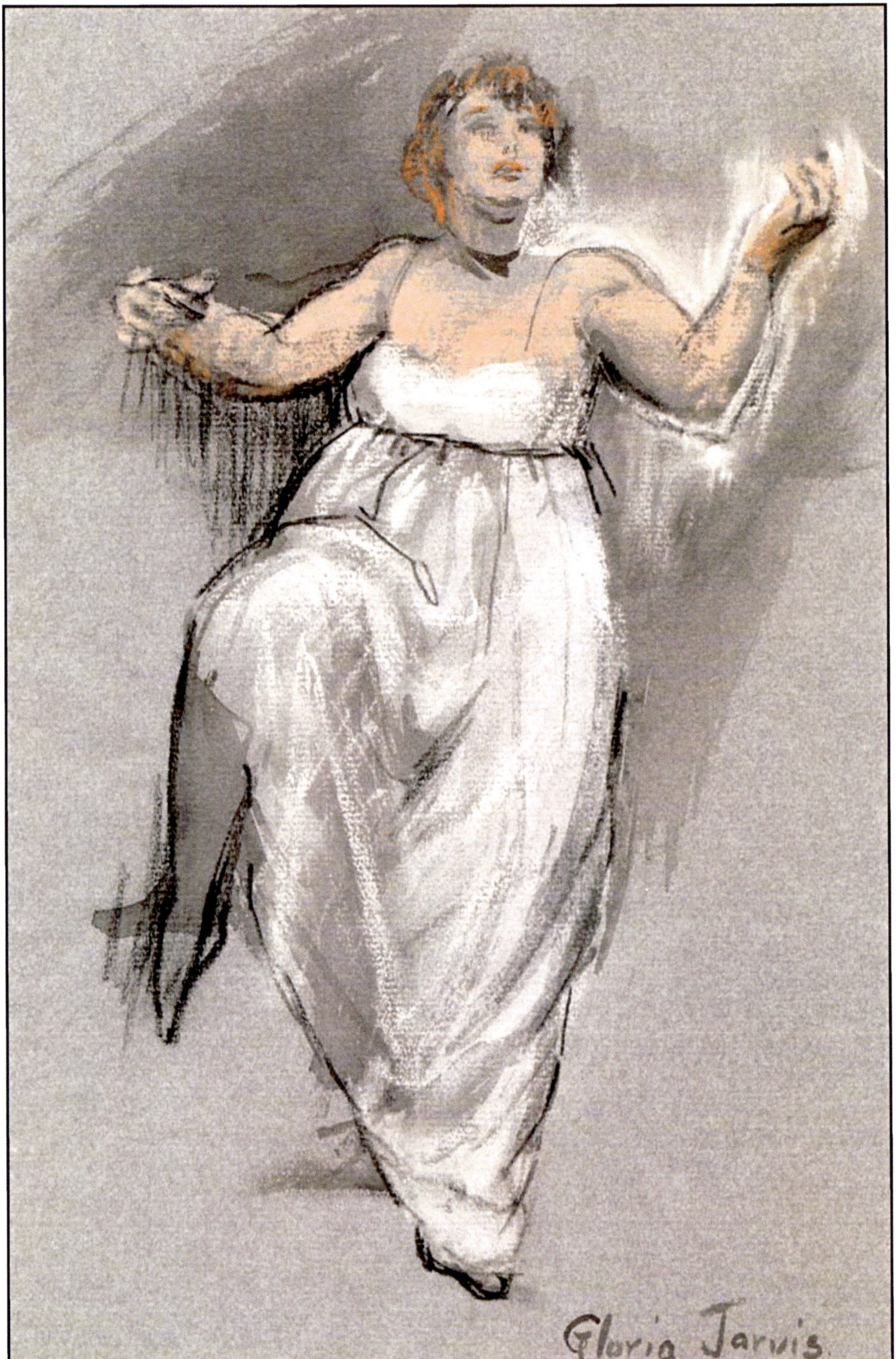
Gloria Jarvis

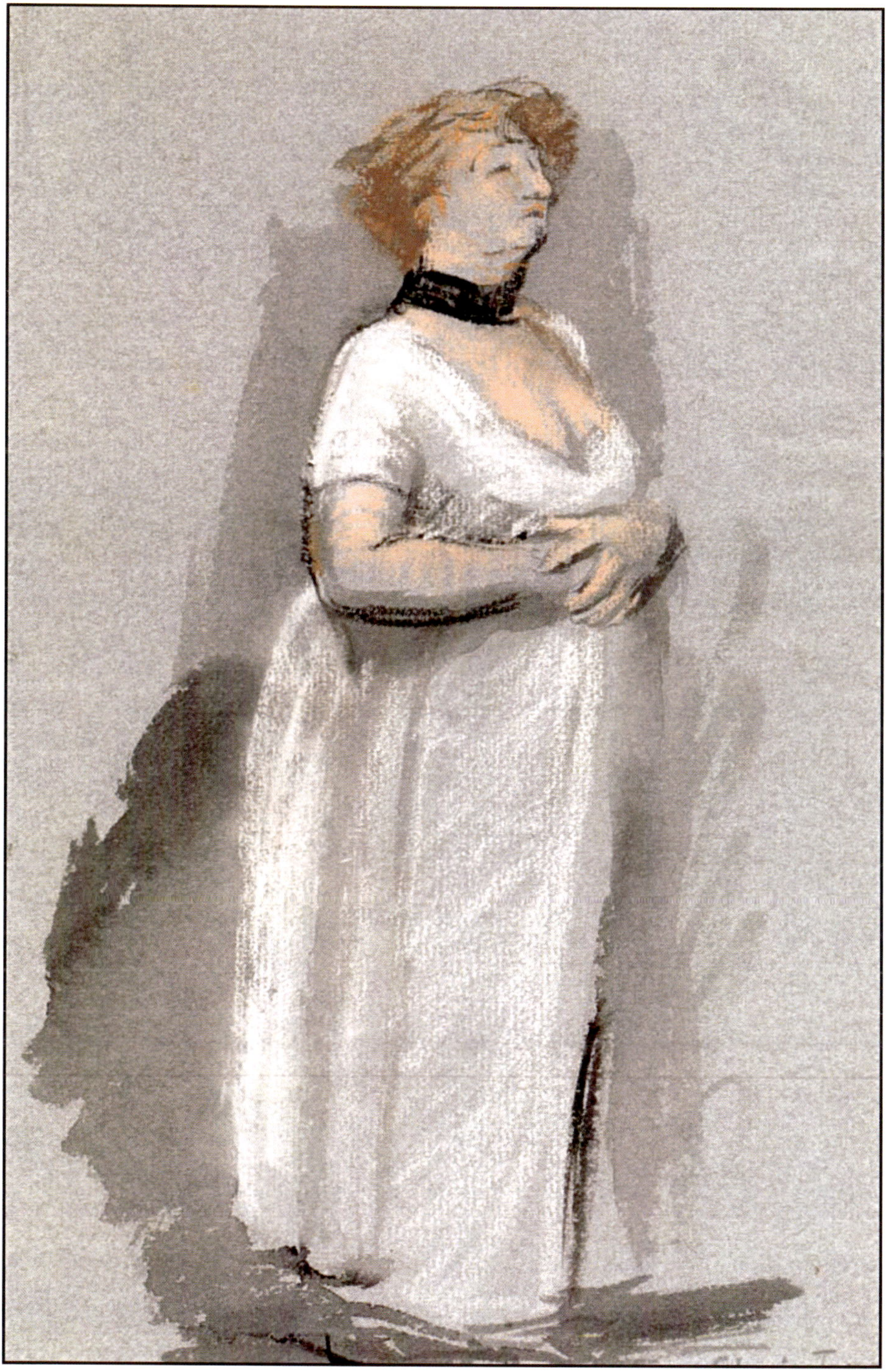

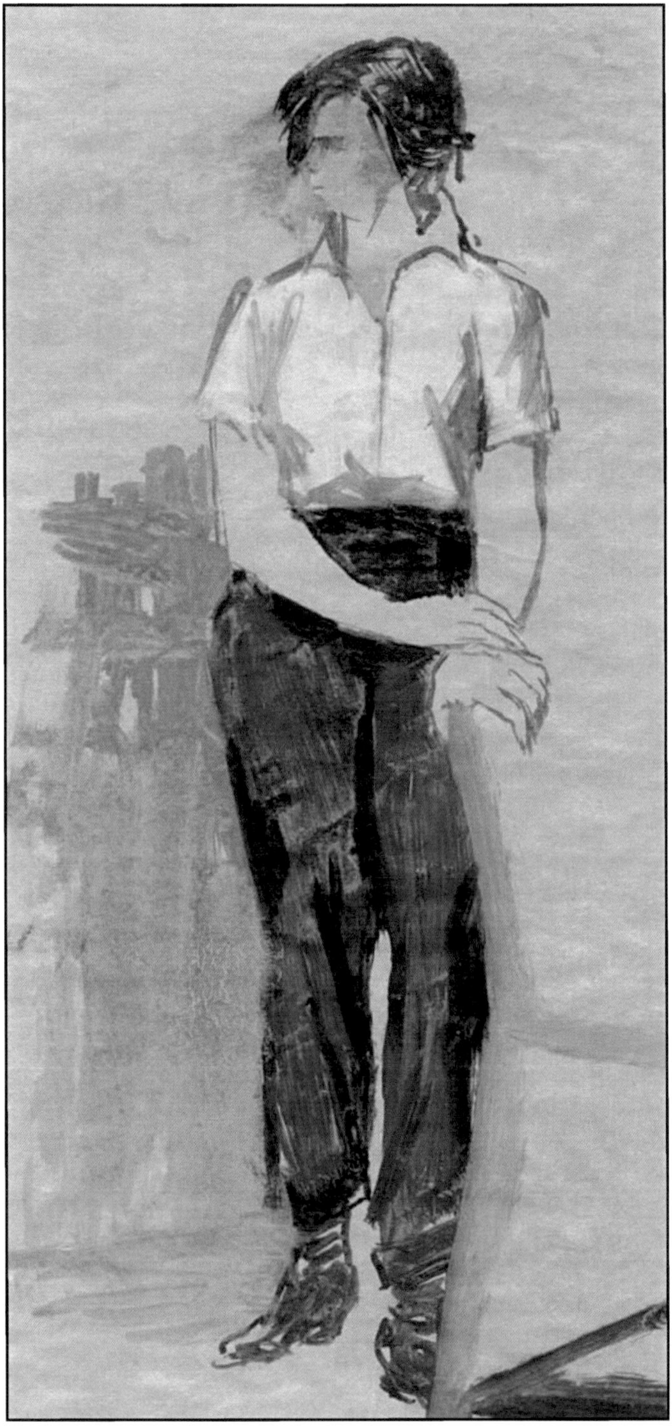

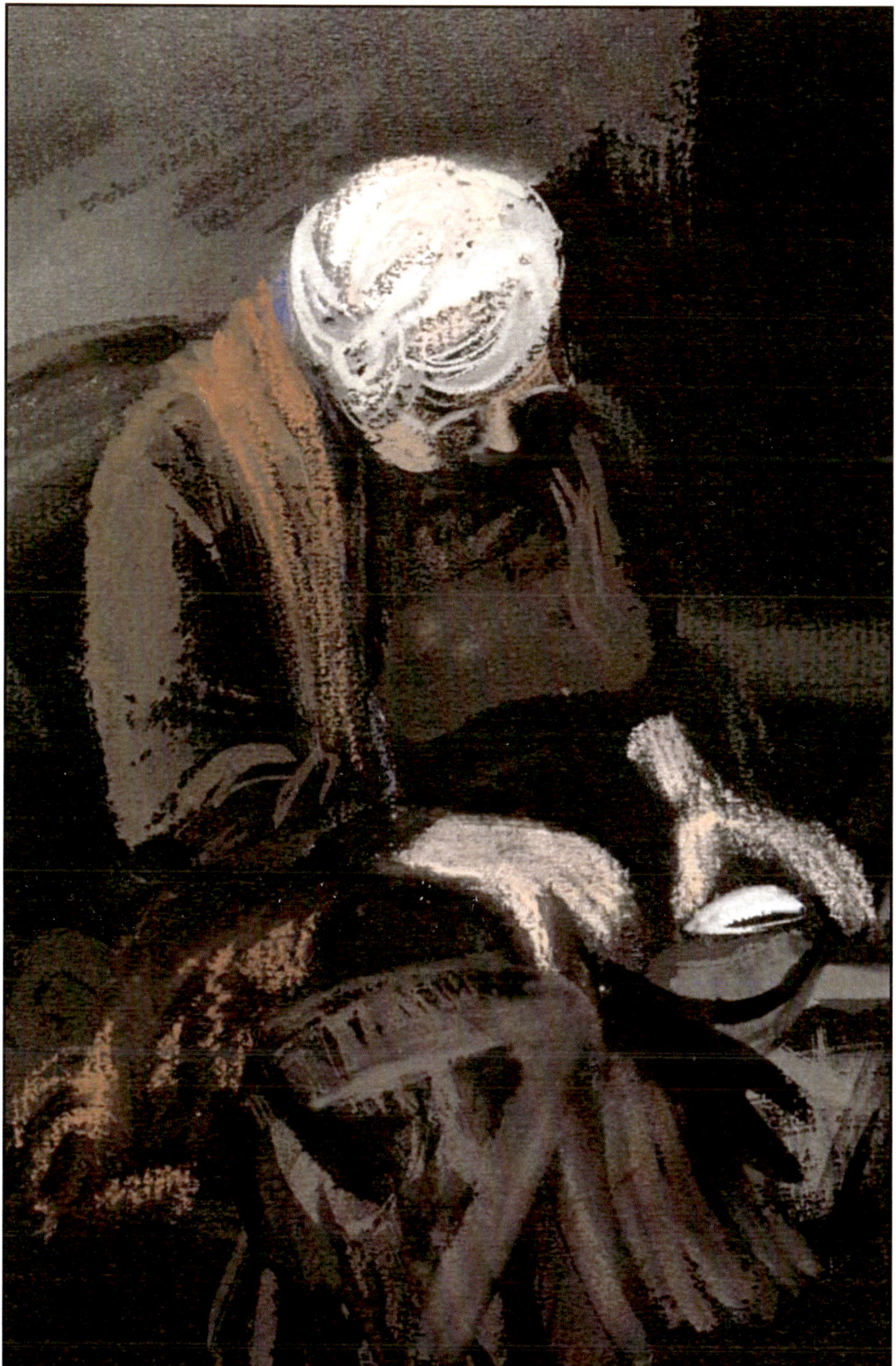

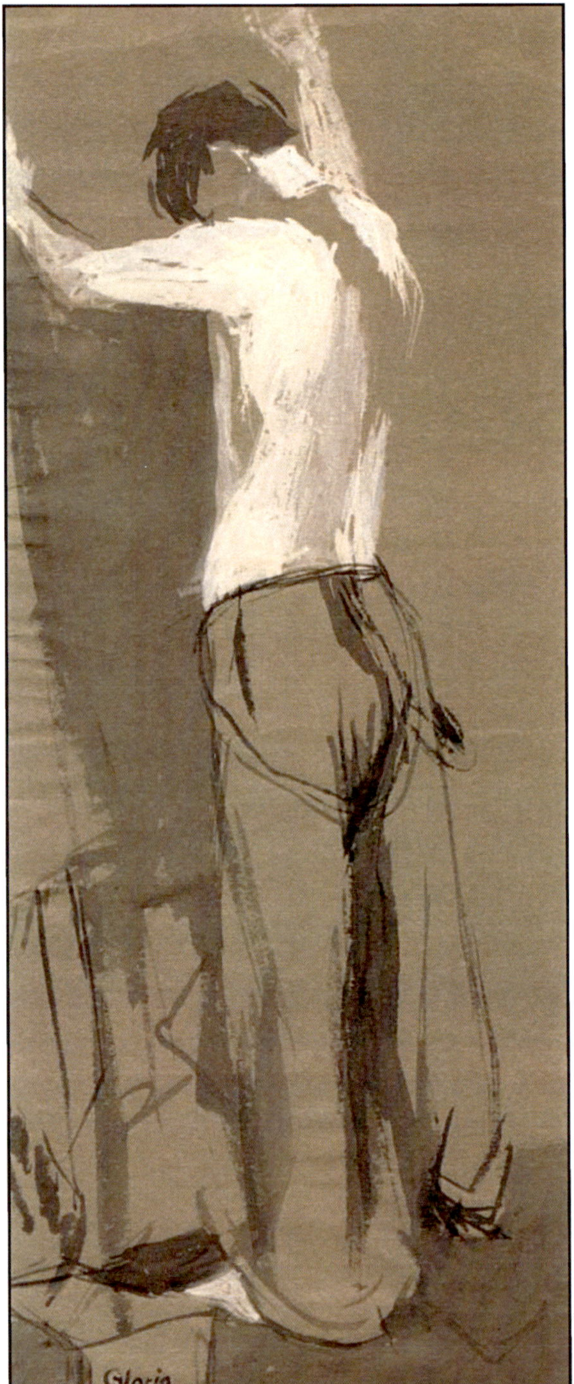
Gloria

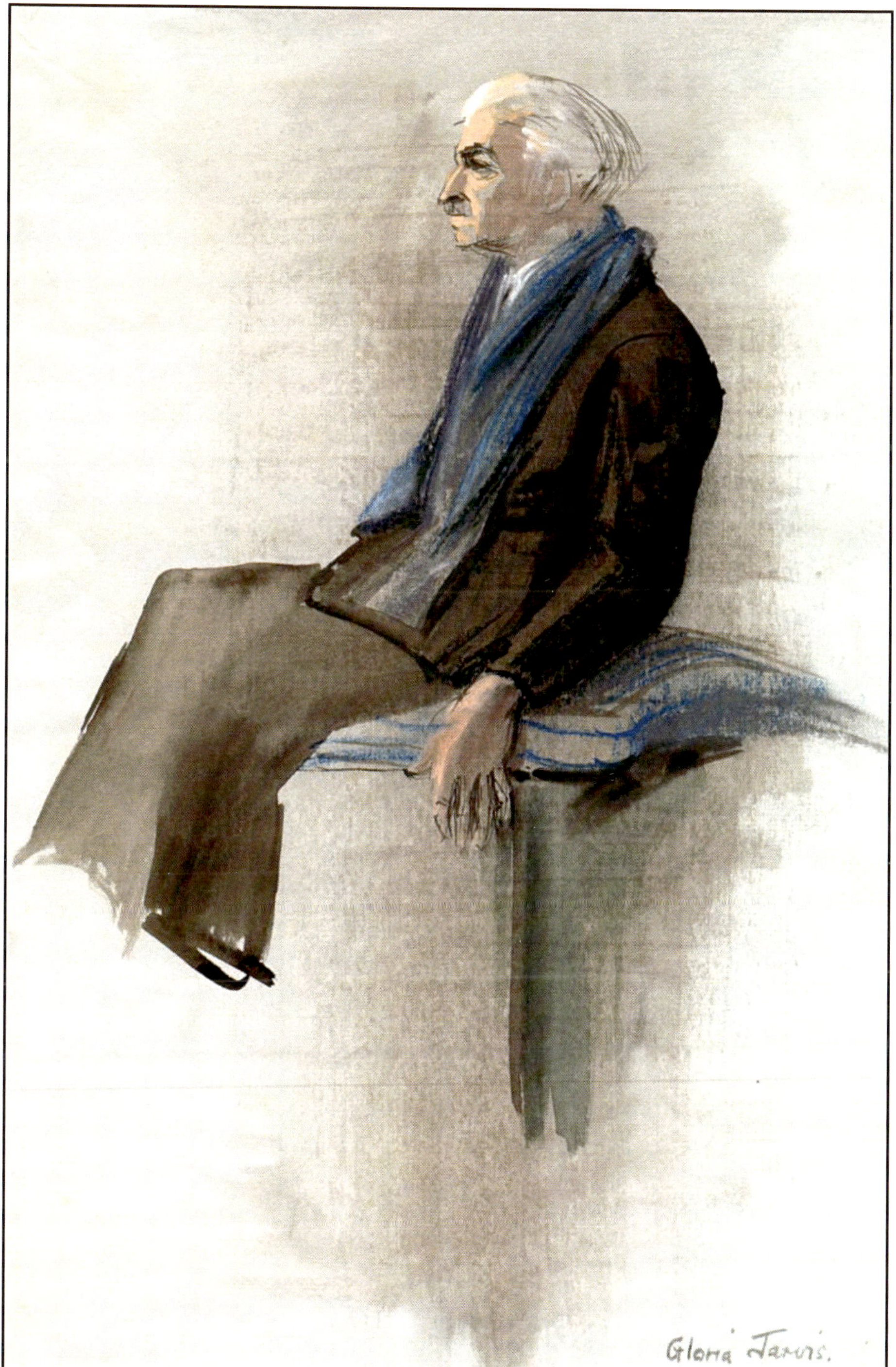
Gloria Jarvis.

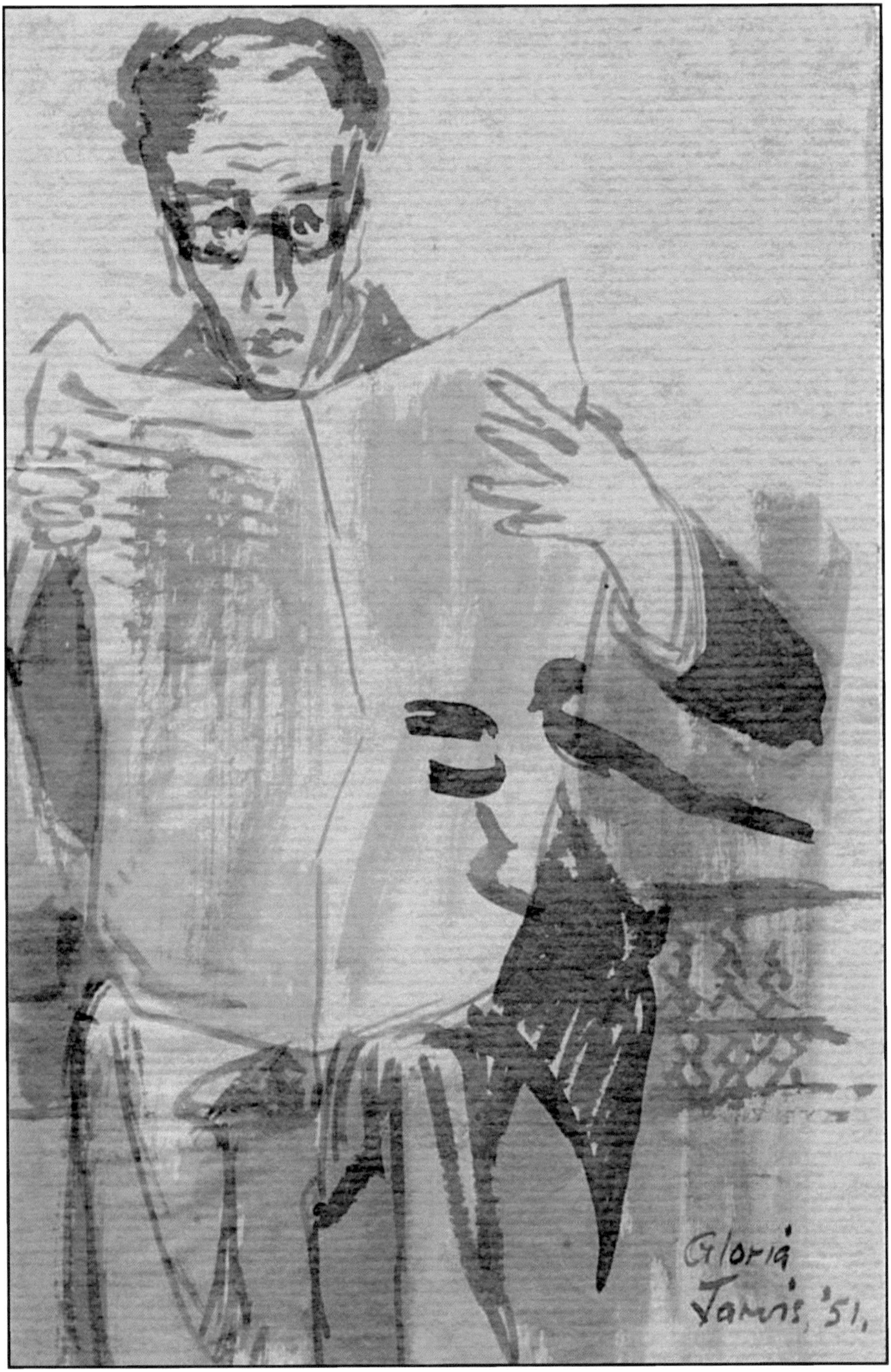
Gloria
Jarvis, '51.

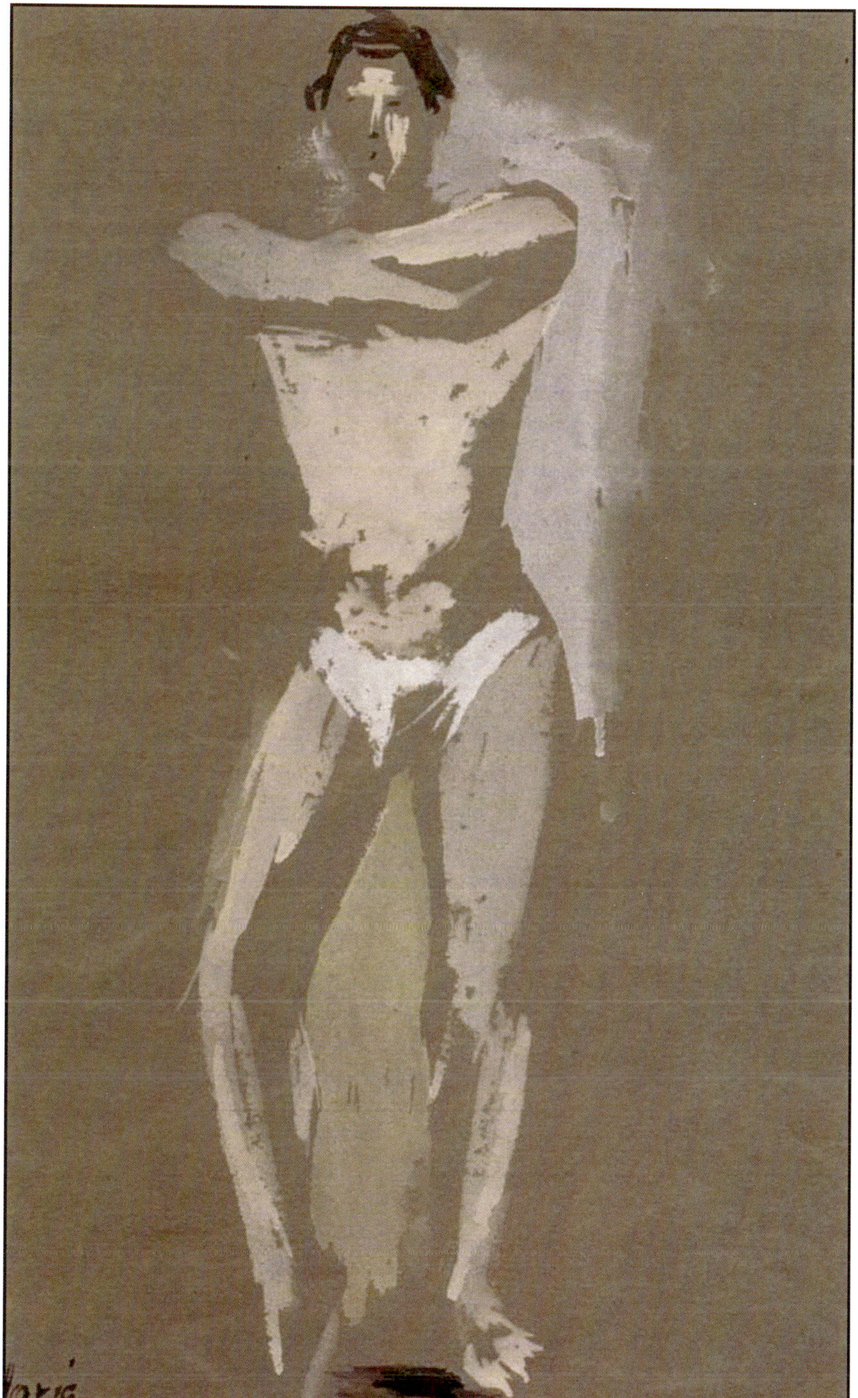

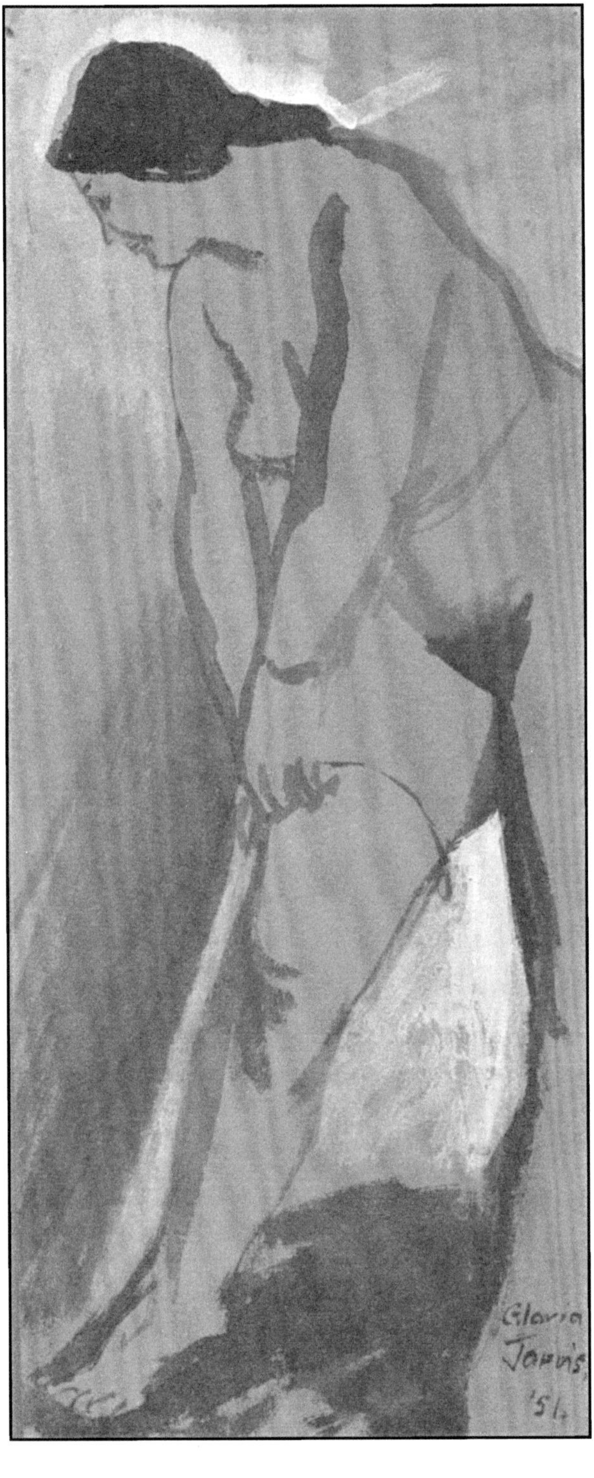
Gloria
Jarvis
'51.

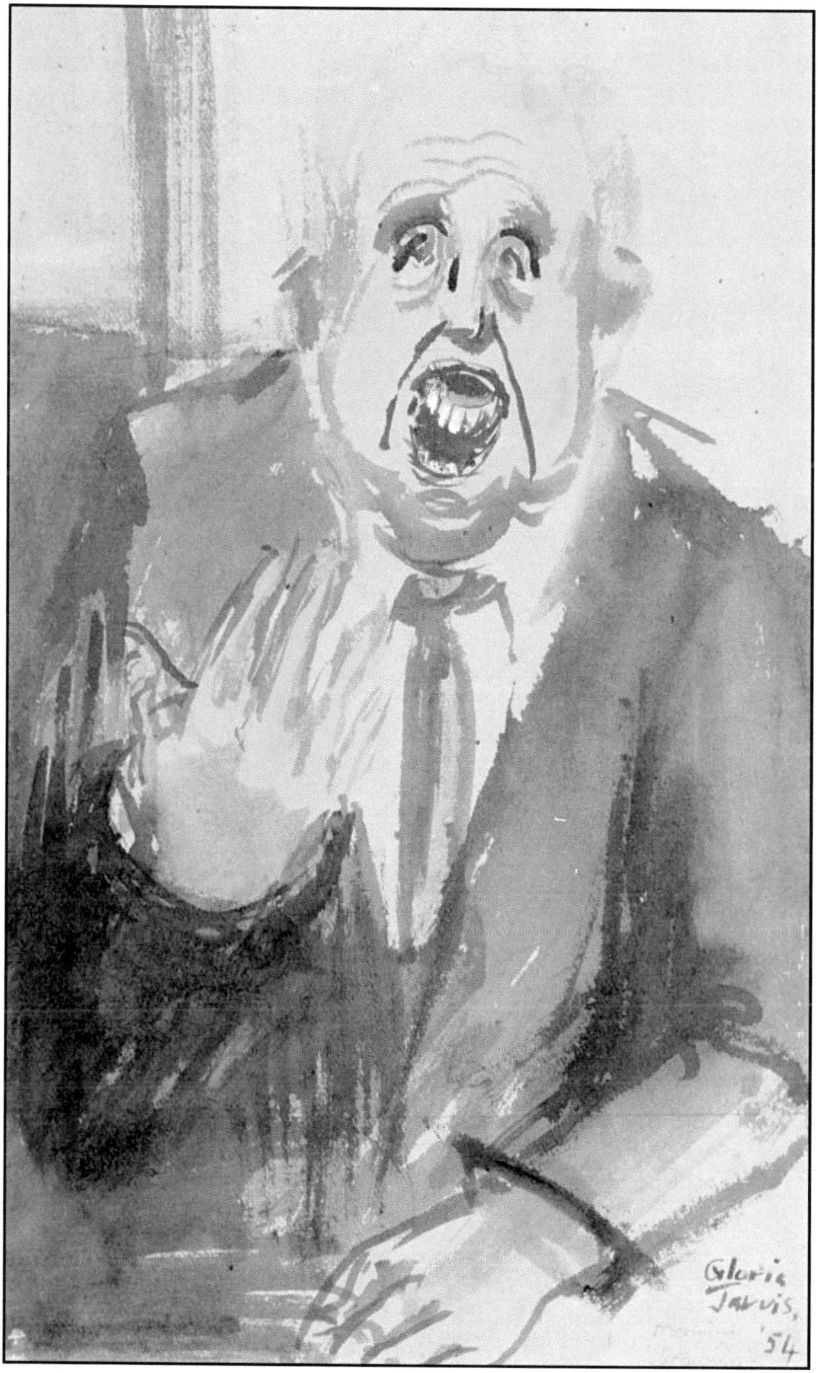

*In the London Underground - his false teeth kept descending.
From memory.*

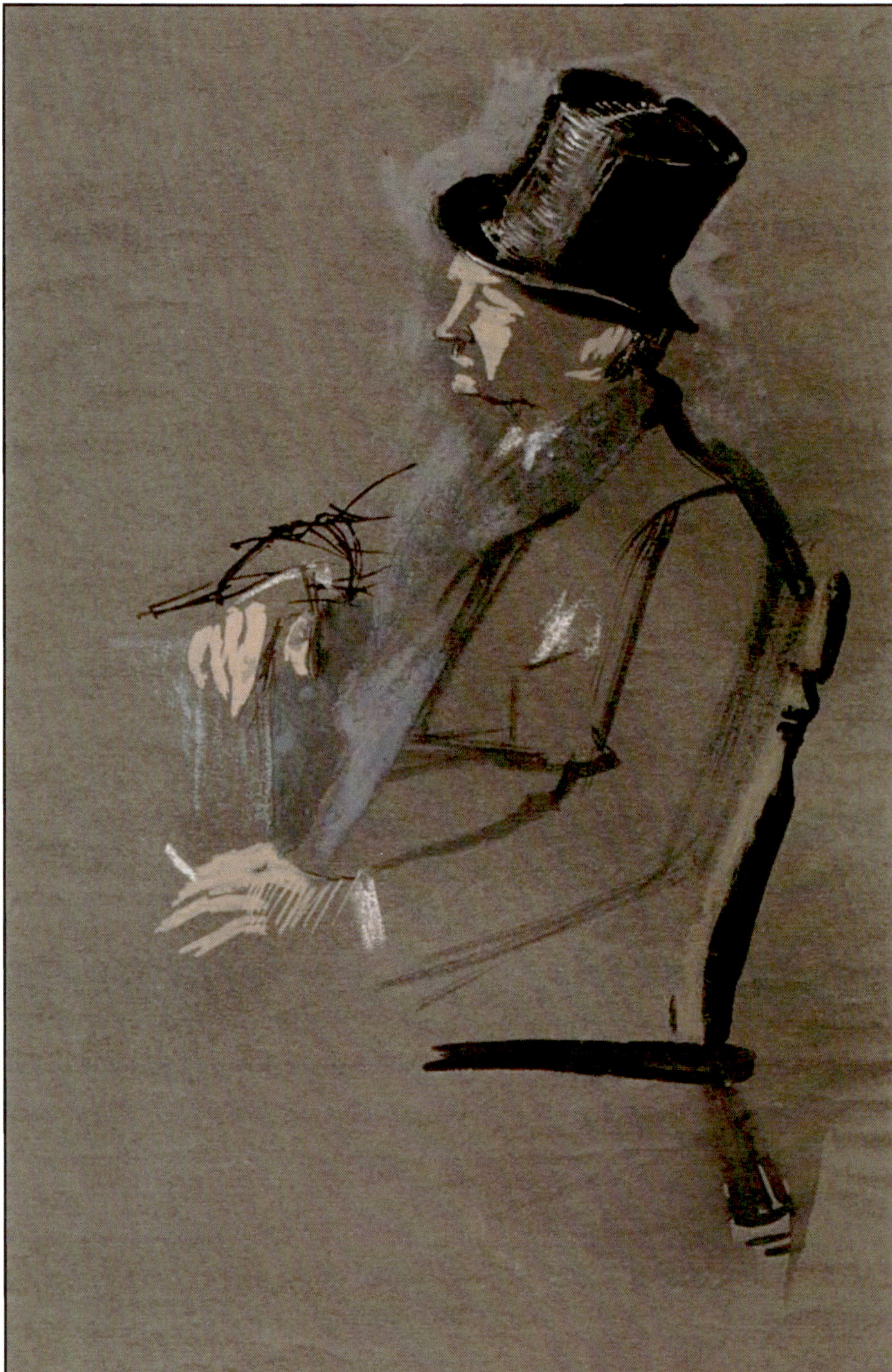

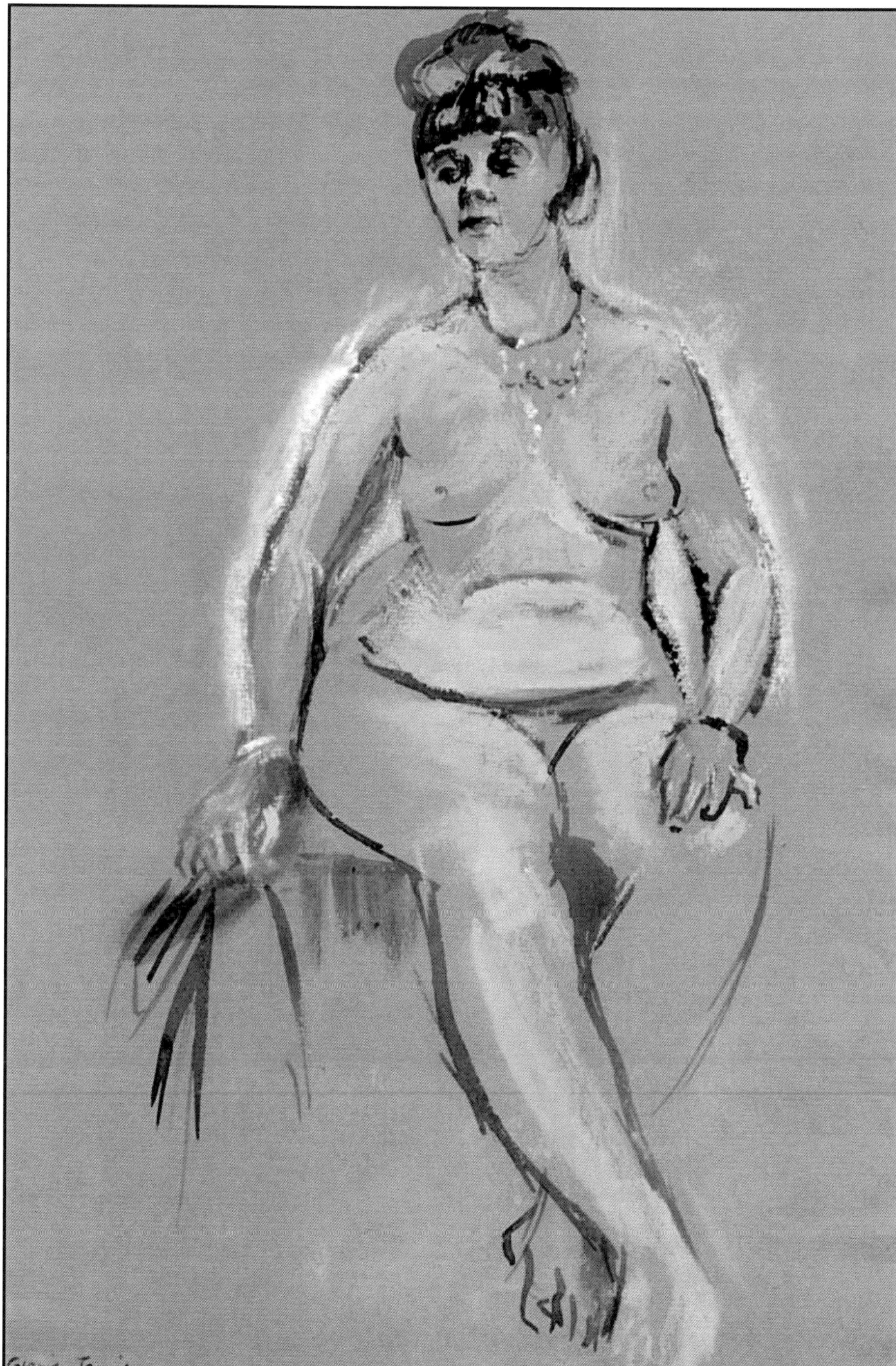
Gloria Jarvis.

Some days Bateman invited us to his studio in Chelsea for the afternoon class to give us a more interesting setting. No. 3, Chelsea Manor Studios in Flood Street was on the ground floor. You entered the little hall, with a strip of Persian rug, a small console table presided over by an inscrutable Buddha under an antique mirror, opposite the Royal Academy's Diploma, framed. Kitchen, bedroom and the usual offices led off the hall, and at the far end you entered the studio proper.

It was immense, with a northern light, filled with an interesting collection of pictures, antique furniture, rugs and objets d'art, for which Bateman had an unerring eye. An Elizabethan tapestry and an Etruscan vase were the most precious of the artefacts.

There were plenty of easels and "donkeys", a sofa and Chippendale chairs. The whole studio made a setting that lent atmosphere.

During the time I assisted my Professor of Painting and Composition, James Bateman, on his commission to paint twelve "Fairs of Britain" for the Whitbread Calendar of 1953, my parents and family all became friends of Jimmy and had an open invitation to drop in on his Chelsea studio.

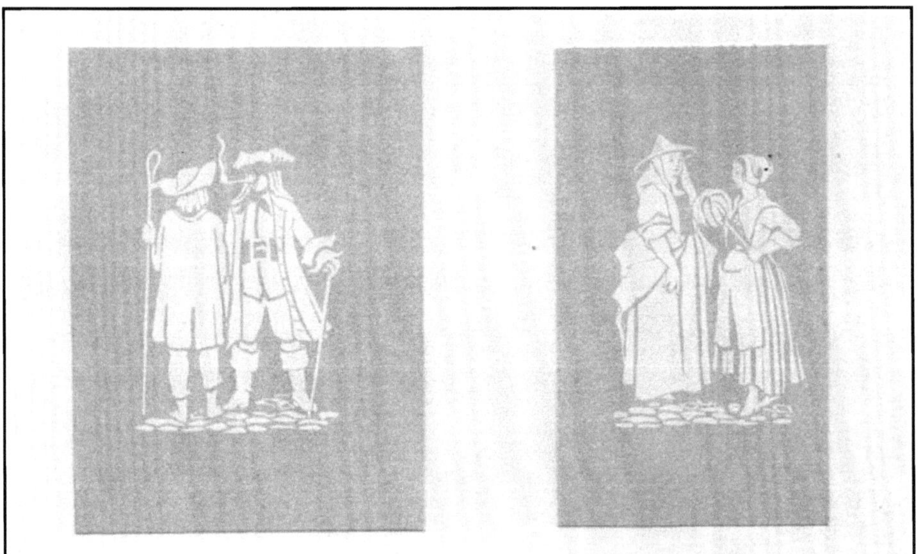

Farmer hiring shepherd *Mistress hiring maid*

Figures in late 17th Century costume at the Mop Fairs.
(Two vignettes for the Whitbread Almanack, 1953)

He could be full of impish fun – in contrast to his serious side – a terrible tease at times.

One evening when my parents and I went over for a drink he suggested they might like to visit a rather unusual venue – sprung on many an unsuspecting visitor – and deliberately planned so as to see how they would react.

It was a basement club in a side street. Down the stairs we trooped and into the local haunt of a roomful of lesbians – quite esoteric in a sensational way for those days – but this was bohemian Chelsea. We came upon a scene of women in various attitudes and modes of behaviour and dress – many in masculine attire (Eton crops and men's suits) – reclining round the room à la Toulouse Lautrec drawings.

Although my father was a man of the world, my mother was such an innocent in those surroundings that she could not contain her fascination with the spectacle before her astonished eyes. In contrast, my father stood with dead pan expression, trying to look as though he hadn't noticed what was going on. Smart in his office suit, with furled umbrella and trilby hat, his reaction went to the other extreme – as he gazed into the middle distance above the heads of the dancers smooching cheek to cheek – as though oblivious to those women my mother couldn't take her eyes off.
How out of place we must have looked! Jimmy and I were hardly able to contain our amusement, which made my father go "ssh!" under his breath, afraid that some of the women might notice and take offence – even pick a quarrel, mistakenly thinking we were laughing at them.

Afterwards, though, away from it all, he could see the funny side, for, in reality, he had a great sense of humour capable of appreciating the comic situation created by our presence – when unconventionality met the conventional.
Was it the Ladies I had gone to – or the Gents, I wonder?

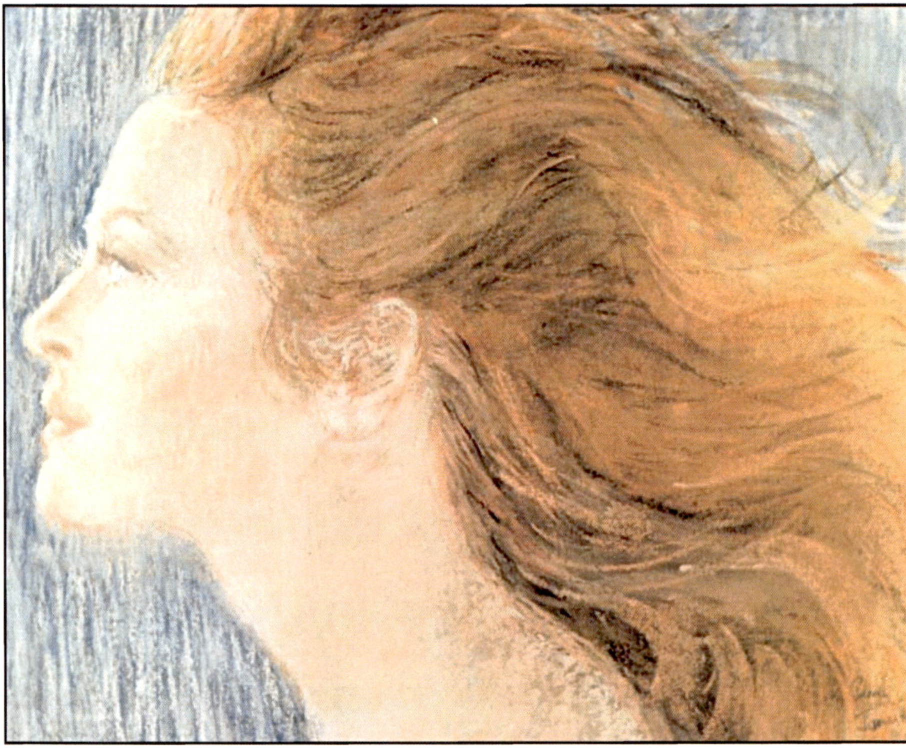

A pastel portrait of Miss Judy Parfitt

A Brush with the Naked Civil Servant

One of the distinctions I can claim is that of having drawn the "Naked Civil Servant", Quentin Crisp, in the life classes at St Martin's. He was, indeed, the King of the Models as I called him – for he was an ace at striking superb poses – full of action – and holding them for 10 minutes or more.

Picked that morning by the tutor from a bevy of waiting models eager to earn an honest penny, when he appeared in class we students set to work with a will. Being paid a fee by London County Council did make him technically a civil servant, and, but for the compulsory jock-strap, he was naked – justifying the title he gave his autobiography in later life.

Although mainly remembered as a broadcaster, for me he will always be the young, enigmatic Quentin we drew, looking across at him from the tiered rows of the life room all those years ago.

After making a flamboyant entrance, with a slight air of indifference, he would sit out of sight behind his disrobing screen over which his trousers would be flung. At length the call from the tutor of "Time, please!" had him kicking off his red high-heeled shoes and bounding onto the dais, a young Adonis, with his shock of hennaed hair. He had said in his autobiography that, at the start of the war, he had bought up a huge consignment of henna in case of a shortage. Two electric fires were placed on the dais to keep him from freezing.

Quick action poses being Quentin's forte, for the next hour until mid-morning, he would go through his paces, lunging and flexing as the minutes sped. There were poses which had the flavour of a Da Vinci notebook of nudes, sketched for some grand design on canvas.

Of course, we guessed he was homosexual which, in those days, if practiced, carried a legal penalty – but students have been ever broadminded, so we did not let it colour our opinion of him. Instead, his silent demeanour intrigued us, for he was withdrawn, a very private individual. This was at odds with his later admitted exhibitionism in his youth. Try as we might we could never coax him into talking.
In his heyday of fame in latter years, it was always my intention to write to him to tell him how highly he was regarded as a model and how much we enjoyed drawing him. Perhaps it is not too late to pay homage, posthumously, to the naked civil servant.

****

After the war young people were at last able to study art and architecture in the galleries and cities of Europe. A brief period in Italy saw me earning an honest lira teaching English. Au pair jobs among Italian families were on the books of the British Council, to whom I addressed myself. But spoilt brats were not the easiest to contend with............

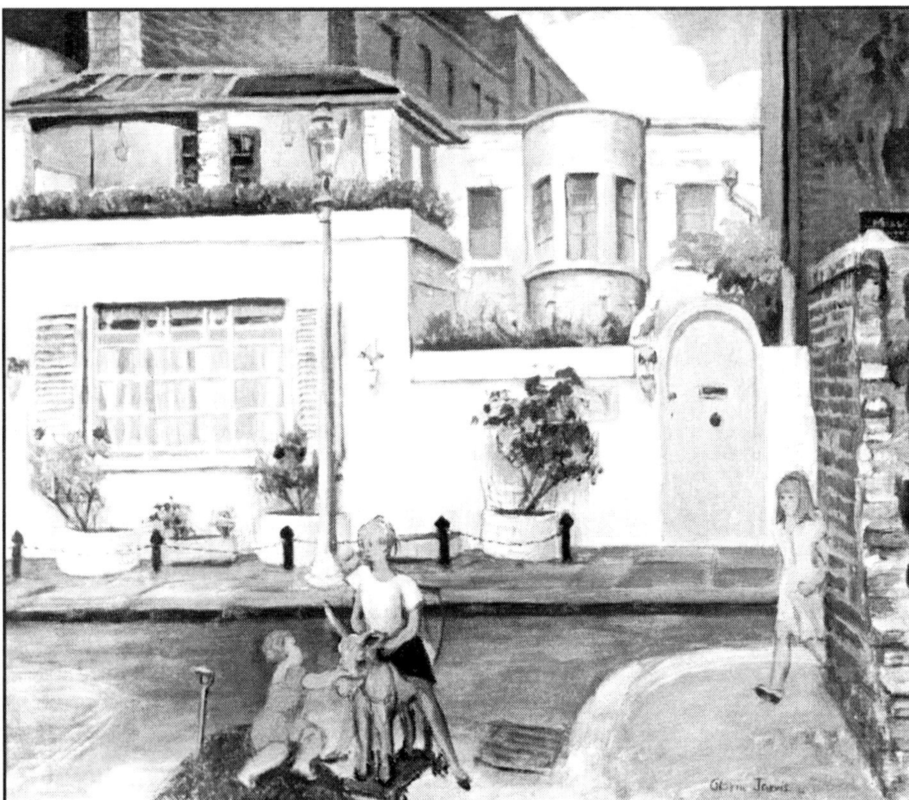

Smith Terrace, Chelsea, London - oil (24" x 20")
In the collection of the artist

Au Pair in a Roman Summer

I had expected an interview with the boy. But his mother's glowing account of him seemed reference enough. The prospect of halcyon days ahead here in Rome – and at the sea – my task merely to exercise a docile child in English decided me. I took the job.

When the two of us did meet, however, his disappointment was as great as mine. This girl was not as pretty as the last au pair, his eyes plainly said. But then, neither did his scowls fit the picture his mamma had painted of him! Swift with his feet - he landed me a kick.

"Be nice to the Signorina," coaxed la mamma. "Why not take her to see your bird?"

The child brightened and led the way through the patio doors and onto the roof garden. But even the breathtaking view across to Santa Trinità and the Spanish Steps could not dispel that air of foreboding. When something near at hand caught my eye: Looming between two beds of lush vegetation stood a massive birdcage, and inside there glowered a big black exotic bird which turned hopping mad at the sight of me, flapping and screeching its rage.

"It doesn't like you," said the child, "and neither do I!".... Something inside me went "doying!" But it was now or never to coax some good will out of the boy and win his trust. Instead, shrugging off all my efforts, he dealt kick after kick after kick.

Suddenly fate took over, as the child on an impulse darted to a garden hose fixed to a tap. Soon he was spraying all and sundry - including me - roaring triumph at the top of his voice, while the bird - a delighted onlooker - screamed its approval, egging him on in his pursuit of me round the plants and bushes. Only by making a dash for the lounge would I get clear of the little fiend.

He anticipated my move. But I fooled him by dodging back in time to escape the cascade of water which rained on the doorway.

In that split second la mamma emerged, dressed for a reception at the Quirinale Palace, and pausing on her way to embrace her sweet little angel. Instead, she got a cold douche full in the face - and figure - she was drenched, as was all her expensive finery! For a moment shock rendered her speechless. Then, letting out a scream of blue murder, she charged. Hell had no fury like this dripping virago launching herself at her erstwhile pet. And as she chased him round that roof garden - hurling shocking insults in English at me for not attempting to control the little brat - I seized my chance and slipped through the open door and across the lounge.

Finding my suitcases where I had left them, I grabbed one in each hand and made for the stairs. Then, bounding downwards, every flight a precious milestone, I reached the street door and fled out into the via Condotti - panting as if from a ghastly nightmare, and thanking my lucky stars to have escaped with nothing worse than a couple of bruised shins and a wringing wet dress!

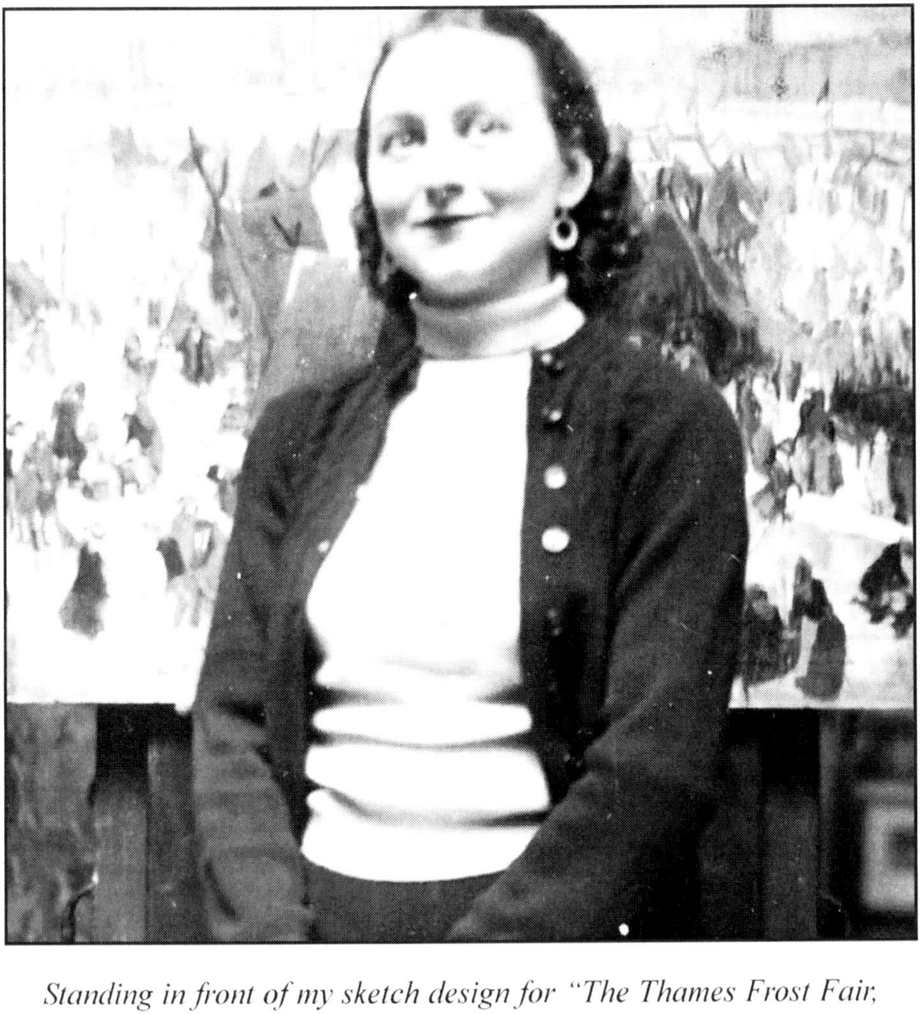

Standing in front of my sketch design for "The Thames Frost Fair, 1740"

“The French” and “The Last Supper”

St Martin’s students of that epoch will remember “the French” round the corner in Old Compton Street. It was considered the thing for anyone with social pretensions to jostle their way into the tiny space, standing room only, to chat at the top of their voice over a cup of strong coffee à la française.

The morning class was punctuated by a break after the first hour. At 11 sharp, models in the life rooms would vacate the dais, don a kimono and flip flop slippers, to join the throng. The hush of the building was shattered by a sudden opening of doors on each floor for the mass exodus down flight after flight to the canteen to join the queue at the hatch for coffee.

Who will ever forget the exceedingly long staff table stretching across the top of the room and dubbed by some wag “The Last Supper” – a parody of Leonardo’s fresco. At the right hand end sat the Principal, urbane and smiling, surrounded on either side by a coterie of tutors in the fine arts who obligingly broke into laughter when called for as the Head waxed witty. And thus the rest of the staff continued down both sides of the table in their respective pecking order.

Students crowding the other tables gossiped – and when election came round – the first after the war – discussed how they were going to vote for the first time in their lives.

Most of the female students got a crush on one or two of the life tutors. Who had not given herself that final preen before stepping into class?

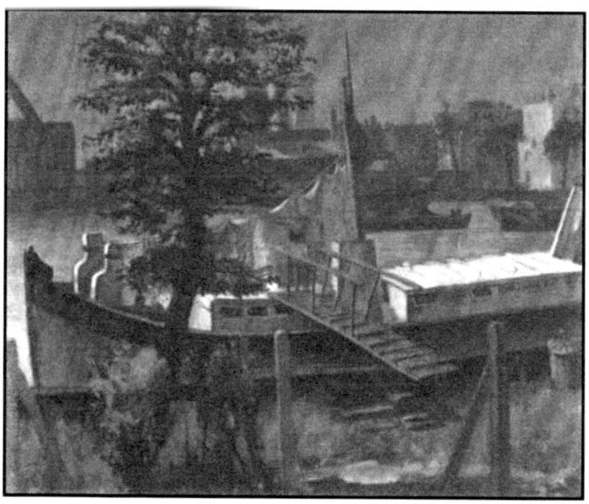

The Thames from Battersea churchyard, 1959
Private collection

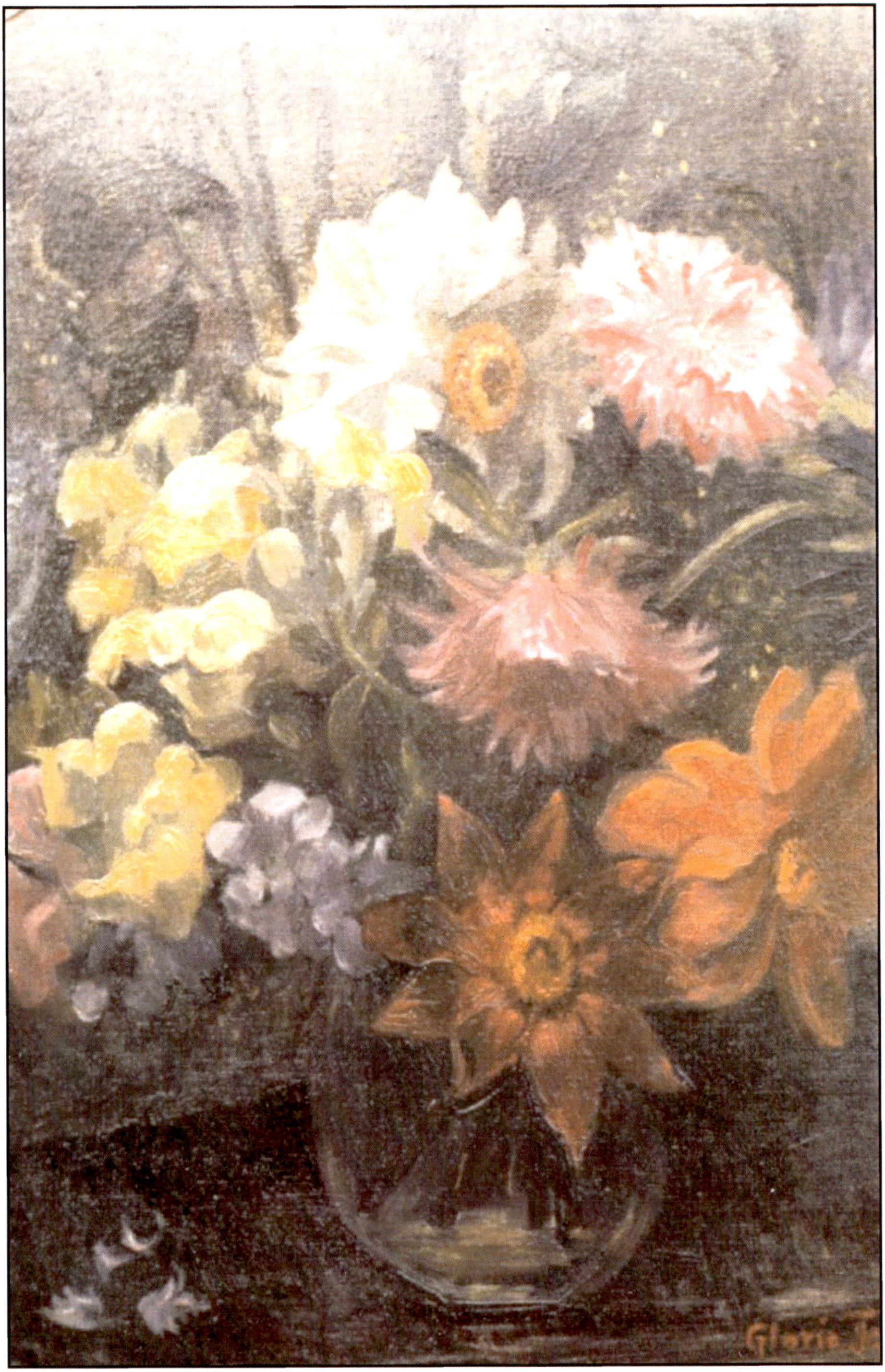

That All-Night Party

"I say, private rooms!" I remarked, indicating the bill board to a friend outside a restaurant we were passing. "It conjures up Edward VII and his mistress, don't you think?"

For the Edwardian public took a permissive society in its stride as long as it was hidden from view – like in a private room. But attitudes were about to change still more. The aftermath of world wars leaves a more lax morality in its wake – what with the "bright young things" of the 1920s; and the 1940 civilians and forces alike were all in it together. Survival was chancy. Attacks from the air could mean you were here today and gone tomorrow. Realisation released inhibitions.

When the Second World War was over, the art school I went to in Soho was packed out with ex-service men and women on grants, who'd acquired varying degrees of "street cred" (as it is now called). Younger folk from suburbia, such as me, and a fellow student, Marti, stood out like the innocents that we were.

Then there was aristocratic Diana – Diana of the Uplands, as she was known from the gossip columns – blond, coming up to maturity with the stamp of having lived – she hadn't been in the forces for nothing!

One day as the life class broke for elevenses, she stretched her arms languorously and announced:

"I think I'll throw a party – an all-night party."

Marti and I were among those invited, which did not impress my mother. Her dark look expressed disapproval. But I set off, just the same; and so did Marti. We met up at Earls Court Underground Station and eventually found Diana's flat down some area steps. The front door was wide open. All and sundry passing by could drift in off the street – and they did.

Once inside, one of them, a sailor in his rating's uniform, approached me, a bottle of gin in his hand, which he poured into two used gin glasses on the mantelpiece. One of these glasses was thrust at me:

"Drink this!" he said.

"Ugh, no!" went through my head staring at the lipstick on the rim, "How unhygienic!" ran my thoughts.

"You're not game like her!" he said, indicating a girl on a divan, being plied with drink, yet had had more than enough already.

The sailor put his lips to the lipsticked glass and downed the contents, then grabbed me as Glen Miller faded into "A Nightingale Sang in Berkley Square". A mental picture of his spotty nose brushing my cheek put me off – like his wandering hands recalling my mother's warning:

"Don't let them maul you about!"

Further advances prompted me to prize myself away, till the determined sailor pushed me onto the now vacant couch. And he got a resounding slap on the jaw for his pains. I left him holding a smarting face. This wasn't his lucky day.

As the evening advanced the place began to look like a scene out of "The Beggar's Opera", the floor covered with canoodling couples that Marti and I picked our way over to get to the front door and some fresh air.

"Isn't it sordid?" we agreed, but it was too late to get a train. So we walked round and round the square.

We eventually found Diana and three boy friends draped a little worse for wear over the kitchen table; at the sight of us Diana declared:

"I'd have danced on the table in the nude if my respectable friends weren't here!"

"Let's see Covent Garden at dawn!" someone said. They rang for a taxi, and Marti and I were bundled in.

The market was all a-bustle, the cafés round about full of market men. One of them was said to read palms. He told me I would live to be "an old, old, lady", which was reassuring.

The next port of call was to be Brighton, but Marti and I just wanted to go home. Bundled into a taxi again, struggling and dragged into Victoria Station to the ticket barrier, we were rescued by a bobby wanting to know what was going on. Marti and I made a dash for the Metropolitan Line stairs, leaving the company to make an adventurous journey to the South Coast minus tickets, which forced them to hide in the lavatories most of the time.

And as I sat in the train to return to suburbia and Harrow-on-the-Hill, I thought of the fun they would have in Brighton; I just wondered if I was missing out!

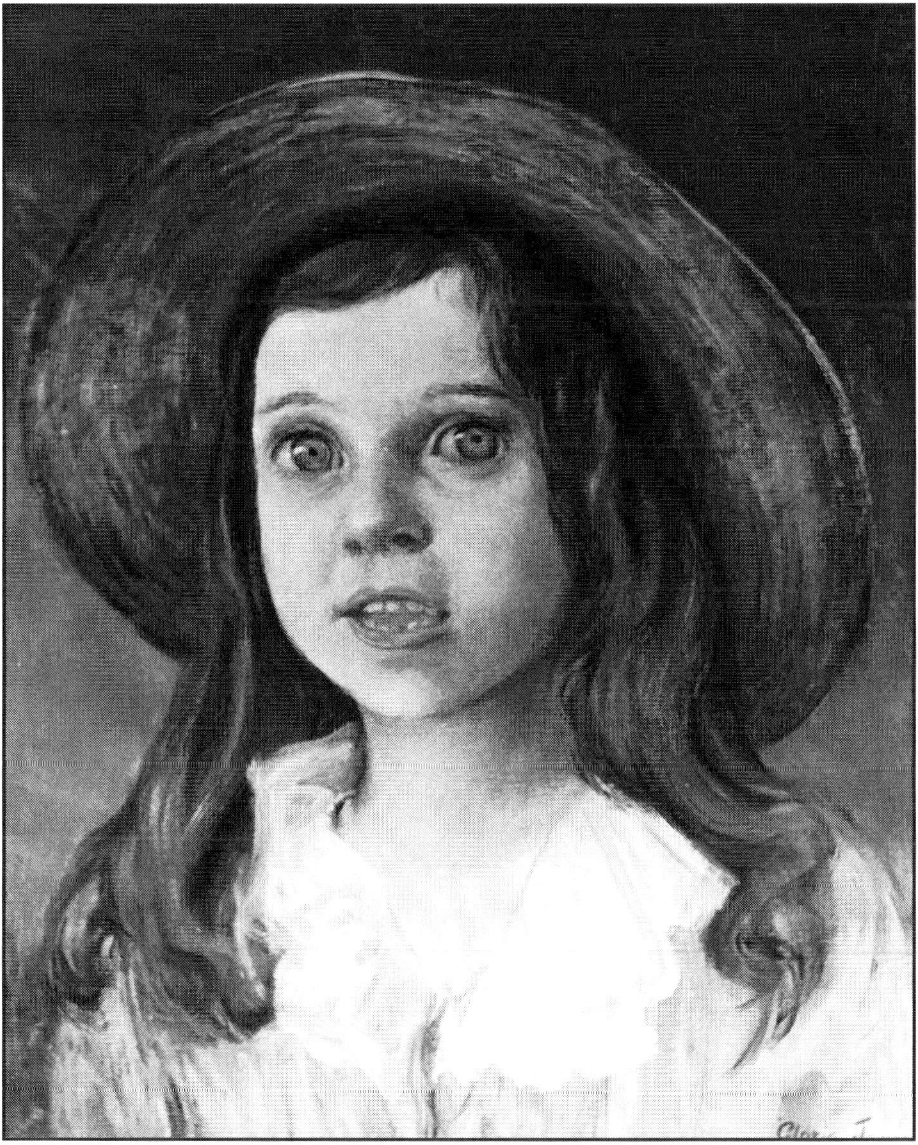

Portrait of a young girl
Private collection

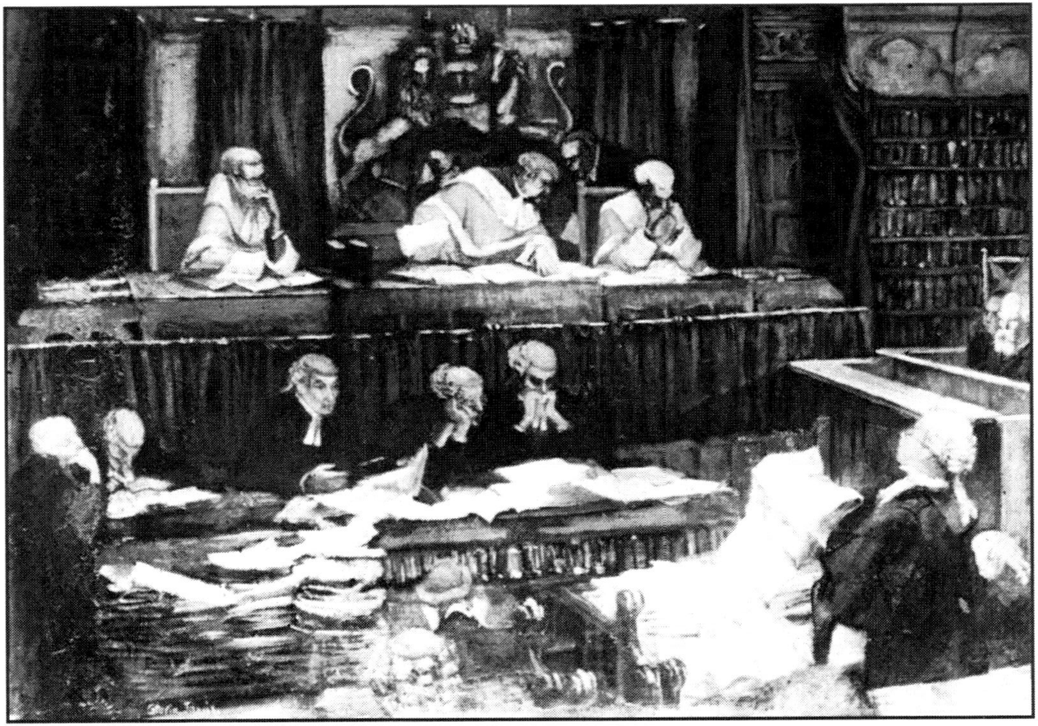

"The Court of Criminal Appeal" in the collection of Maitre Motte de Raedt, Brussels. 85" x 55" oil. Executed in the mid 1950's. It shows the appeal against his conviction for murder of the Polish farmer. Nicknamed by the press "Mr Whiskers" (on the right). Lord Goddard, the Lord Chief Justice is the central appeal judge.

The Train to Lucca

Thanks to understanding parents, my student days at St Martin's stretched into nine years. I was helped, too, by the award of a scholarship from the London County Council. Then after gaining the National Diploma in Painting and Design I was ready to apply for a job to teach art. One of the senior tutors, Vivian Pitchforth, nudged me, and with a wink, joked: "All set for a little council school in Wigan?" – not knowing I had been applying to the London art schools, having set my sights higher.

I counted myself lucky to be appointed Lecturer on Historic Costume at Hammersmith School of Art and Regent Street Polytechnic, where I also taught Drawing from the Costume Model – in fact, I continued to teach at Regent Street for twelve years, except for an intervening year's sabbatical in Florence studying the History of Art. While there I took the opportunity of looking up some of my Italian relatives not far away.

The train to Lucca made the first step on the journey to the enchanting hill town where they lived: Fornacci di Barga, high up, above Viareggio, but inland.

Lucca stands out in my memory as the place where I learned to pronounce "tea" properly in Italian. It was in a small bar in the Renaissance square. The whole family emerged to try and make out what my insipid "tay" meant. Then it dawned on them – and on me – as they gave the correct way to rap it out as a very brief rap indeed. Since then I have taken great pride in rapping out: "te" – with stress on the letter "t" – the rest is just a breath of sound.

Back at Lucca station I boarded the rail connection for the climb up to that beauty spot, Fornacci di Barga, atop this unspoilt countryside. As one ravishing view succeeded another, my thoughts were racing ahead to the imminent meeting with relatives whom I knew only vaguely smiling out of photos – or as names spoken by my mother, their cousin.

Clotilda, my grandmother Dizolina's sister, was long since dead, but Florrie, another sister, lived there with her family – while Giulia, the unmarried niece, looked after the old father, known as Santucci.

Under Mussolini he had been mayor of Fornacci, but loyalty to the Fascist party meant his being stripped of mayoral status after the war. As a respected citizen, however, he was allowed to keep his house – on pain of fine, as penalty for his past. Regarded by the family as a bit of a tyrant, especially to Giulia who danced attendance, he watched me keenly, with head held back à la Mussolini – so that he appeared to be looking down his nose at me. But to my grandmother's surprise, when I told her back in England, he rose at crack of dawn the next day to wave me off to catch my train. He had left his four-poster bed with its comforts and ornate lace coverlet so early to keep me company at breakfast – which I took as a proof of welcome, as well as an unselfish act.

In fact the whole family opened their arms to me and we spent a convivial evening round the dining table in Florrie's kitchen, tucking into a meal of dishes all' Italiano. There was no language barrier as they nearly all spoke English – Florrie and Giulia had worked in London in the 1930s.

"Pontings!" said Giulia, pointing out the heavy lace curtains in Santucci's house. That was the store in Kensington High Street, renowned for its furnishing and dress fabrics.

Giulia, of whom I had become very fond, saw me to the station. On the way she acknowledged, in passing, a dark skinned lass – the result of a rape, she said, by one of the Maroccan soldiers sweeping up the Tuscan coast as part of the liberating armies during the war. Her mother was too late to make her escape with the other inhabitants to the hills, like Santucci and kin. They had hidden in a cave until the Maroccans had moved on. They had commandeered all the houses in Fornacci. Once the men in the family had ventured back after dark, and creeping close to the lighted windows of their house, glimpsed a group of Maroccans playing cards round the kitchen table. Once in residence again they found all their blankets and woollen clothes had been stolen. Liberation had not always been a cause for joy.

So it was back to Florence to resume the course on art history I was following at the University given by Mina Gregori, deputy tutor to the Head of Department, the renowned professor, Roberto Longhi. I still have a large exercise book packed with my notes in Italian – proof of my fluency at the time. How rusty one can get in the meantime without constant practice! Mina Gregori was lecturing on the Mannerist painters who threw the necks of their portraits into shadow, making it a mannerism; another day might be devoted to Gothic sculpture, characterised by the slim, attenuated lines of their human forms, arms pressed to the sides, devoid of gesture. Some of the best lectures I have ever attended I had the good fortune to follow there.

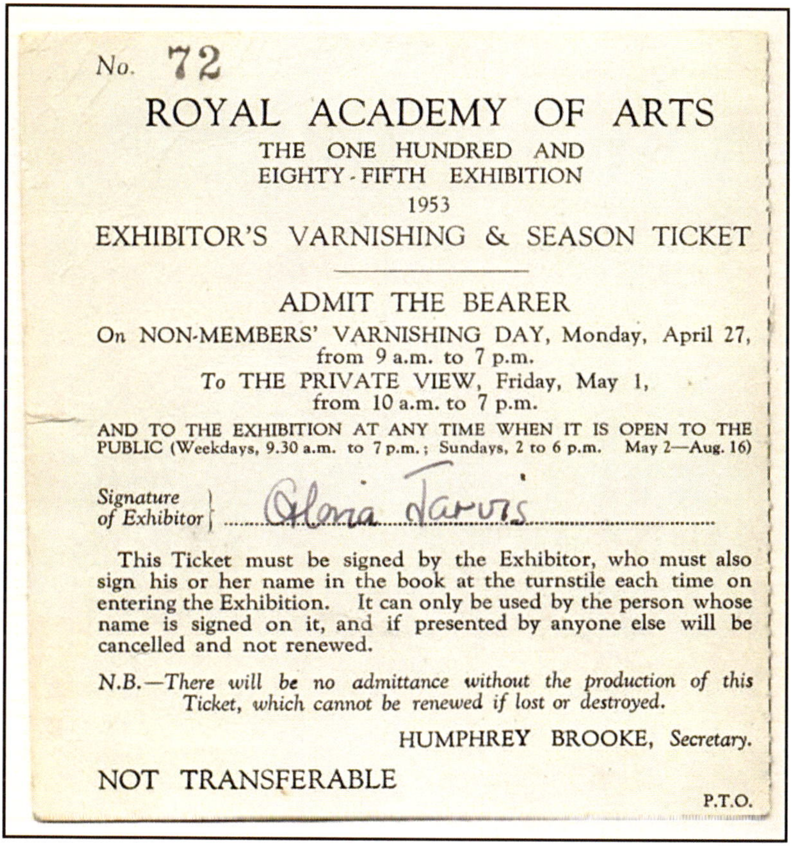

No. 72

ROYAL ACADEMY OF ARTS

THE ONE HUNDRED AND
EIGHTY-FIFTH EXHIBITION

1953

EXHIBITOR'S VARNISHING & SEASON TICKET

ADMIT THE BEARER

On NON-MEMBERS' VARNISHING DAY, Monday, April 27,
from 9 a.m. to 7 p.m.

To THE PRIVATE VIEW, Friday, May 1,
from 10 a.m. to 7 p.m.

AND TO THE EXHIBITION AT ANY TIME WHEN IT IS OPEN TO THE PUBLIC (Weekdays, 9.30 a.m. to 7 p.m.; Sundays, 2 to 6 p.m. May 2—Aug. 16)

Signature of Exhibitor } Gloria Jarvis

This Ticket must be signed by the Exhibitor, who must also sign his or her name in the book at the turnstile each time on entering the Exhibition. It can only be used by the person whose name is signed on it, and if presented by anyone else will be cancelled and not renewed.

N.B.—There will be no admittance without the production of this Ticket, which cannot be renewed if lost or destroyed.

HUMPHREY BROOKE, *Secretary.*

NOT TRANSFERABLE

P.T.O.

GALLERY No. X

OIL PAINTINGS—(Nos. 505–570)

505 The Fur Hat .. .. *M. B. Critchlow*
506 Thames Frost Fair, 1740 .. .. *Gloria Jarvis*
507 Christ Carrying the Cross .. .. *Robert J. Steele*
508 Portrait of the Artist .. .. .. *Penelope A. Pipe*
509 Athene Seyler as Mrs. Trapes in "The Beggars' Opera" .. .. *Maurice Codner*
510 Winter .. .. *Ethelbert White*
511 Mrs. Henry Freedman .. .. .. *Flora Lion*
512 Carnations and Pinks .. .. *Edward Le Bas*, A.
513 Hugh Hield, Esq. .. ..*Reginald G. Brundrit*, R.A.
514 Charlotte, 1953.. .. .. .. *Edward I. Halliday*
515 Spring Morning .. .. *Rosalie Loveday*
516 Regale Lily and Orchids.. .. .. *Amy Watt*
517 September Evening .. .. *Algernon Newton*, R.A.
518 Sir Thomas Beecham, Bt. The National Tribute for his outstanding services to Music. *Simon Elwes*

Atlas Holding Up The World Of Regent Street Poly

Atlas, the Titan, with the global world on his shoulders, covered a good part of the mosaic floor of the spacious foyer of Regent Street Polytechnic, just over the way from Broadcasting House. It was familiar ground I walked over for the best part of twelve years, every Monday and Wednesday, plus two evenings a week, when I was teaching in the School of Art on the top floor, 1950-62.

It wasn't till after I'd left that this mosaic on a grand scale I learned had been executed by my Italian grandfather, a master craftsman in mosaic when he had his London business pre-Second World War.

A centrally situated polytechnic in London's West End was bustling with students – my evening costume classes in particular – as the area round Oxford Street was the centre of the rag trade. But I look back on my day class with affection – a select band of young men and women studying illustration – when my demonstrations with methods of drawing in different media came in useful.

The evening students were mainly in the fashion industry, employed in small businesses – in Carnaby Street, for example – working as machinists but aspiring to be dress designers and aiming to put their ideas on paper. In September, at the start of the school year, I would have about 40 students or more. It was a challenge trying to get round to as many as possible in the allotted two and a half hours as they drew from the costume model; and I would get quite a few black looks from those, perforce, left out.

Many were refugees: a German Jewish woman astonished me with her remark, "Germany will rise again, just you see!" It was the note of triumph in her voice that shook me, considering how the Jews had been treated.

During the 1960s the School of Art in Regent Street Polytechnic ceased to exist when it was amalgamated with Chelsea School of Art. But by that time I had married Ray Smith. We had moved over to the Continent where he was better employed using his linguistic qualifications as interpreter and translator.

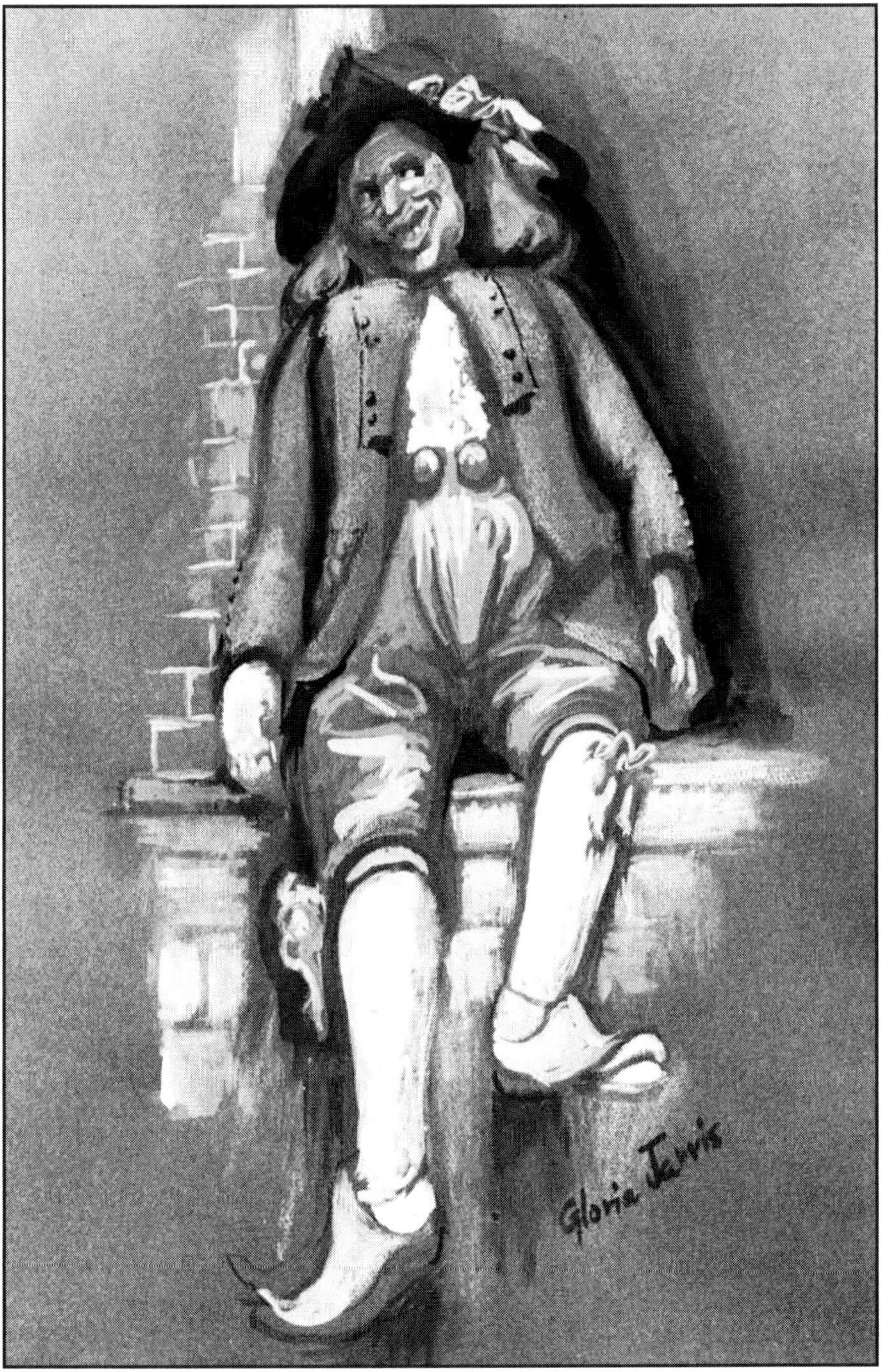

A Marionette from the Théatre de Toone - Brussels
drawing in pastel and gouache - private collection

BRUSSELS

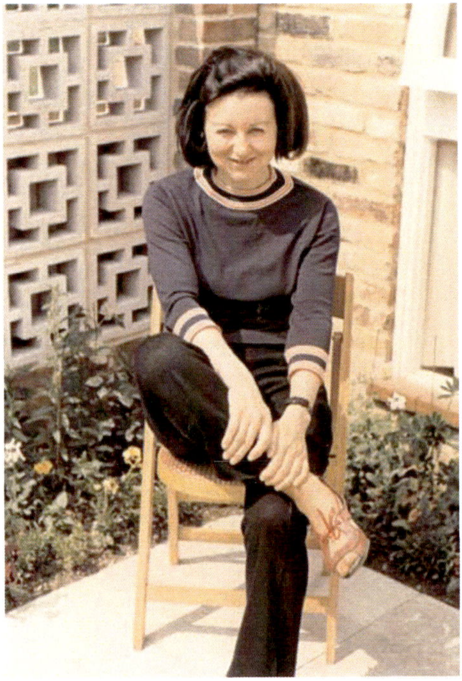

"In compiling this book I have been able to see much of my work coming together in one piece. It also forms a trilogy with the two histories of my family: "A Jarvis Tapestry" (parts 1 & 2).

Fate, in taking me to Brussels, launched me into portraiture and the most prolific period of my painting life (until then, compositions and genre subjects, in taking me longer to accomplish, had entailed a slower output).

Besides, Belgians are an art-orientated public and avid exhibitiongoers - my one woman shows afforded me the happiest period of my life - certainly my painting life."

"The Beacon" 14.3.80

GLORIA JARVIS – THE WAY SHE SEE THINGS

Preview

Gloria Jarvis, the English painter well-known for depicting Belgian scenes and personalities, is exhibiting in the hall of the Winterthur Center, 56 avenue des Arts, from 10th to 29th March.

Those who have seen her previous shows will remember particularly those compositions of folklore such as the Haguettes of Malmédy, the Chinels and the Gilles, the marionnettes of Toone. In the field of portraiture, who can forget her rivetting interpretation of Maurice Béjart ? Then there are her reconstructions of the Place de Brouckère — Fin de Siècle, and the Grand-Place peopled with 18th century folk diverted by a troupe of Italian comedians. (All the compositions of Gloria Jarvis are entirely original).

Smaller, intimate drawings come into the less expensive category, though I must say, that for an artist of her calibre, the price range of the whole exhibition is very reasonable. « I prefer to reach a wide public, » Gloria Jarvis says, « And have my work circulating ». This is something she has achieved to good measure, and much of her work has found its way into many important private collections in Belgium and England. She went on to say how lucky she was to be just old enough to have benefitted from studying under some of the great contempories of Augustus John.

A pupil of James Bateman, R.A., who was taught by Sickert and Wilson Steer, she profitted greatly from his teaching of Composition and his ability to nurture his student's vision. This was in the heyday of St. Martin's School of Art in London's Charing Cross Road. There, too, she attended the Life and Costume Classes of Robin Guthrie, who helped her acquire that direct and free handling of the brush distinctive of her work. It is this draughtmanship that is so characteristic of her pictures.

Chinese ink, gouache, pastel, charcoal are media which particularly suit her style, though she is just as accomplished in oil.

Gloria Jarvis has also designed and executed some magnificent screens which are on view in her current exhibition. « Nowadays, screens are rarely needed as draught excluders », she told me, « Instead, people buy them to use as pure decoration to divide a room, or screen off the television ; they also hang them on the wall as triptychs ».

By a directness, spontaneity, freedom of brushwork, Gloria Jarvis expresses the original way she sees things with fine technical accomplishment.

I can heartily recommend you to go and see for yourself. G. B.

CALEDONIAN SOCIETY OF BRUSSELS

The society has now started it's 1979/80 Season for country dancing and meets every Wednesday in the Maison des Ailes, 1, rue Montoyer, Brussels at 8 p.m.

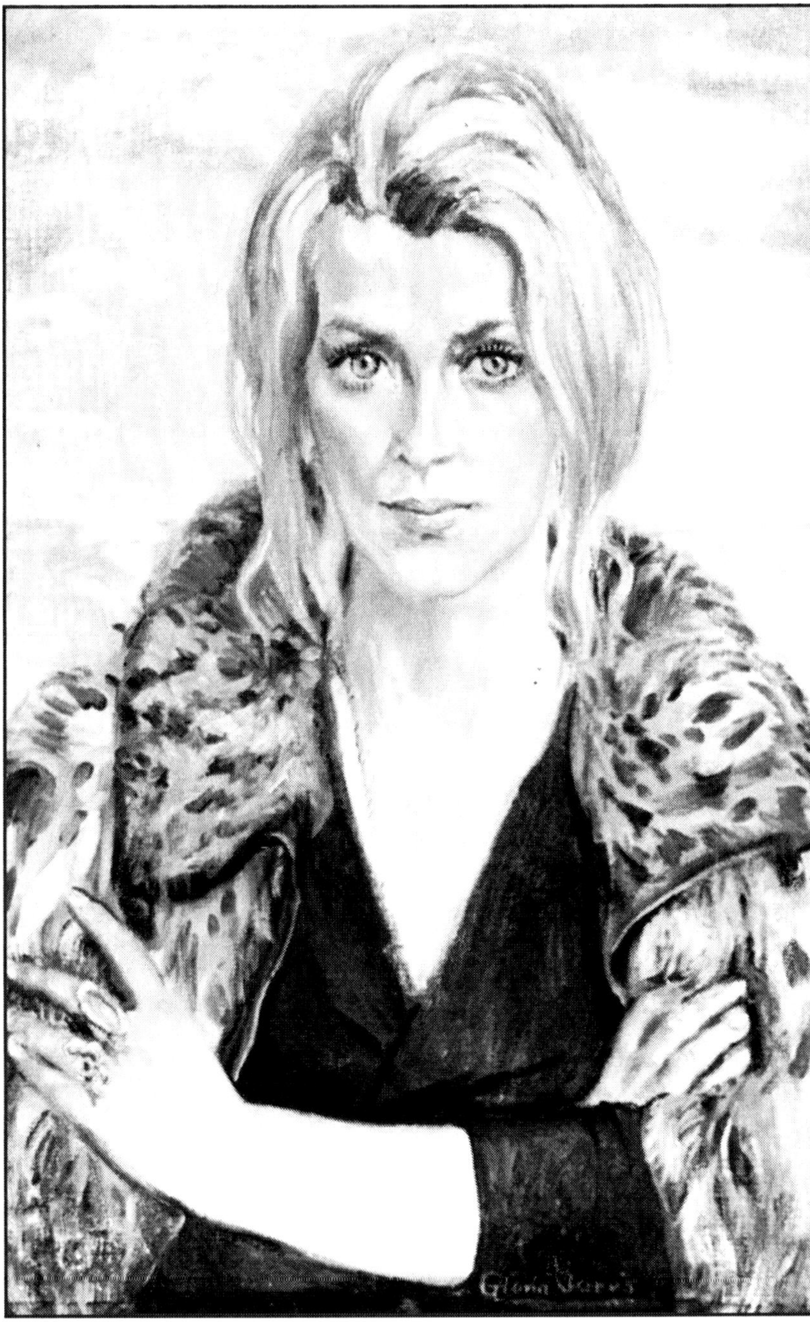

Madame Marie Badoux

Paintings in a Louis Quinze Salon

Old England department store was housed in one of the 18th century palaces in the Place Royale. On high ground, and resembling Fortnum and Mason in style, it seemed to be looking down disdainfully from its aristocratic quarter onto the lower part of Brussels below with its Medieval squares and streets and commercial rue Neuve.

In each of the multiple, wide, street level windows one sole garment elegantly placed lent such a chic air – it made one a little shy of stepping inside the emporium where the equally chic young woman working the lift tended to eye one critically up and down.
It was here I brought my paintings to show the Manager with a view to exhibiting them on a sale or return basis – with portrait commissions thrown in – à la Harrods of Knightsbridge.

Monsieur Godon was enthusiastic. It happened he had once attended art school himself, so had a feeling for painting. The spring fashion shows were about to take place in the salons, and he proposed it as the setting for exhibiting my paintings and drawings – which were duly hung under the judicious eye of the store decoratrice, Marie Badoux. Becoming friends as we did meant that "tea time" in her studio was established as a ritual, where the daily brewing of tea – and one of the scrumptious tarts from a patisserie – were enthusiastically received.

Badoux, as she was known, had the decorative displays of the shop and seven windows to design, and her large studio had an atmosphere of creativity, full of interesting props, as if for the stage. She, herself, based her appearance on that of Catherine Deneuve, the French actress she was said to resemble (my portrait of her opposite is for the reader to judge).

My work on the walls of the salons of Old England continued as a permanent feature, attracting many portrait commissions. For this, it was important to impress on the public that I was capable of capturing a resemblance to the sitter. Thus, I constructed a portrait or two of well-known public figures such as Princess Paola, whose loveliness shone out from all the magazine covers. But my portrait of her was not a copy of anyone of these photos – it was painted from a synthesis of several.
Another such portrait done expressly to persuade the public of its likeness to the subject was that of Churchill – and although the Order of the Garter was bestowed on him not till later in life than depicted in my painting, I nevertheless allowed myself artistic licence. It was bought by a Belgian courier for Sotheby's, New York.

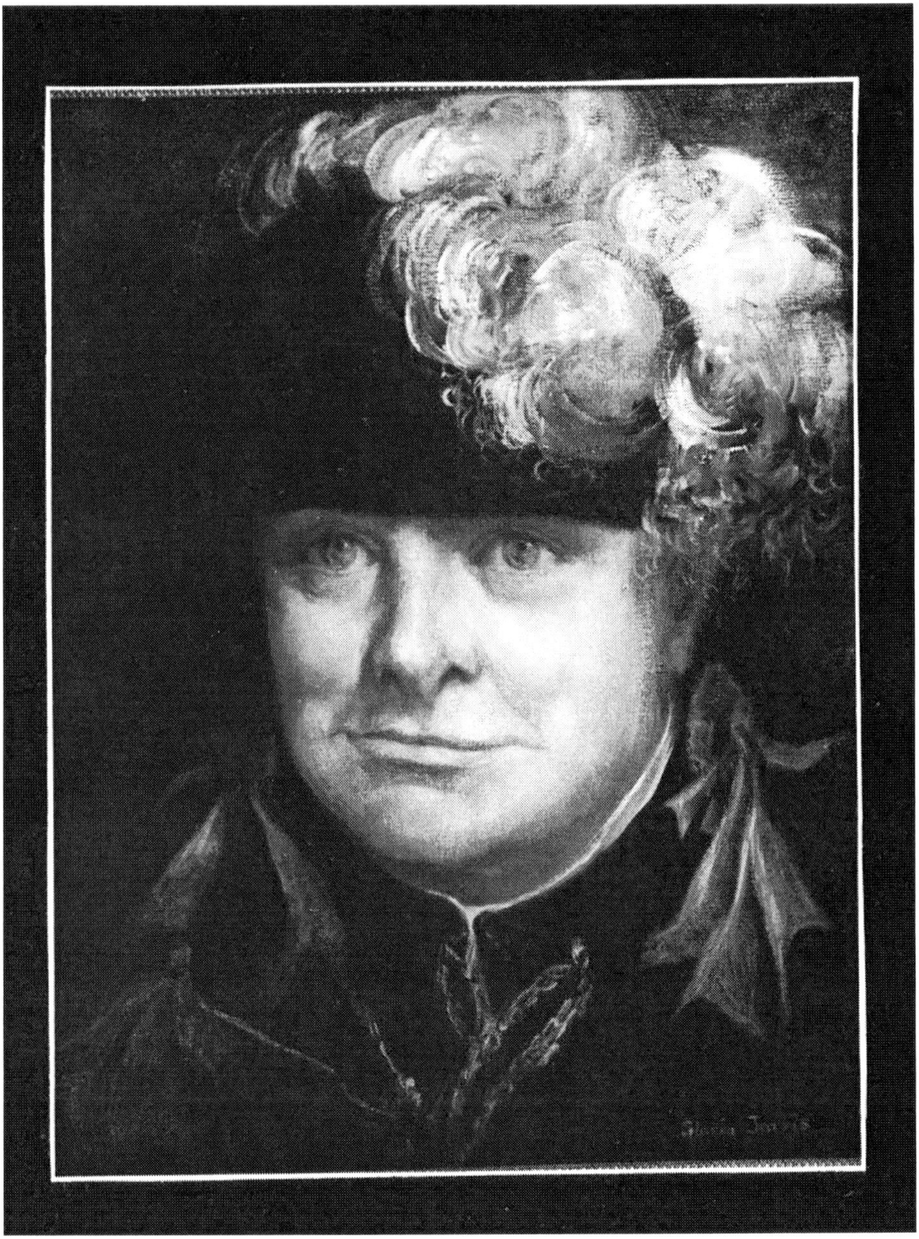

Winston Churchill - private collection
Posthumous portrait

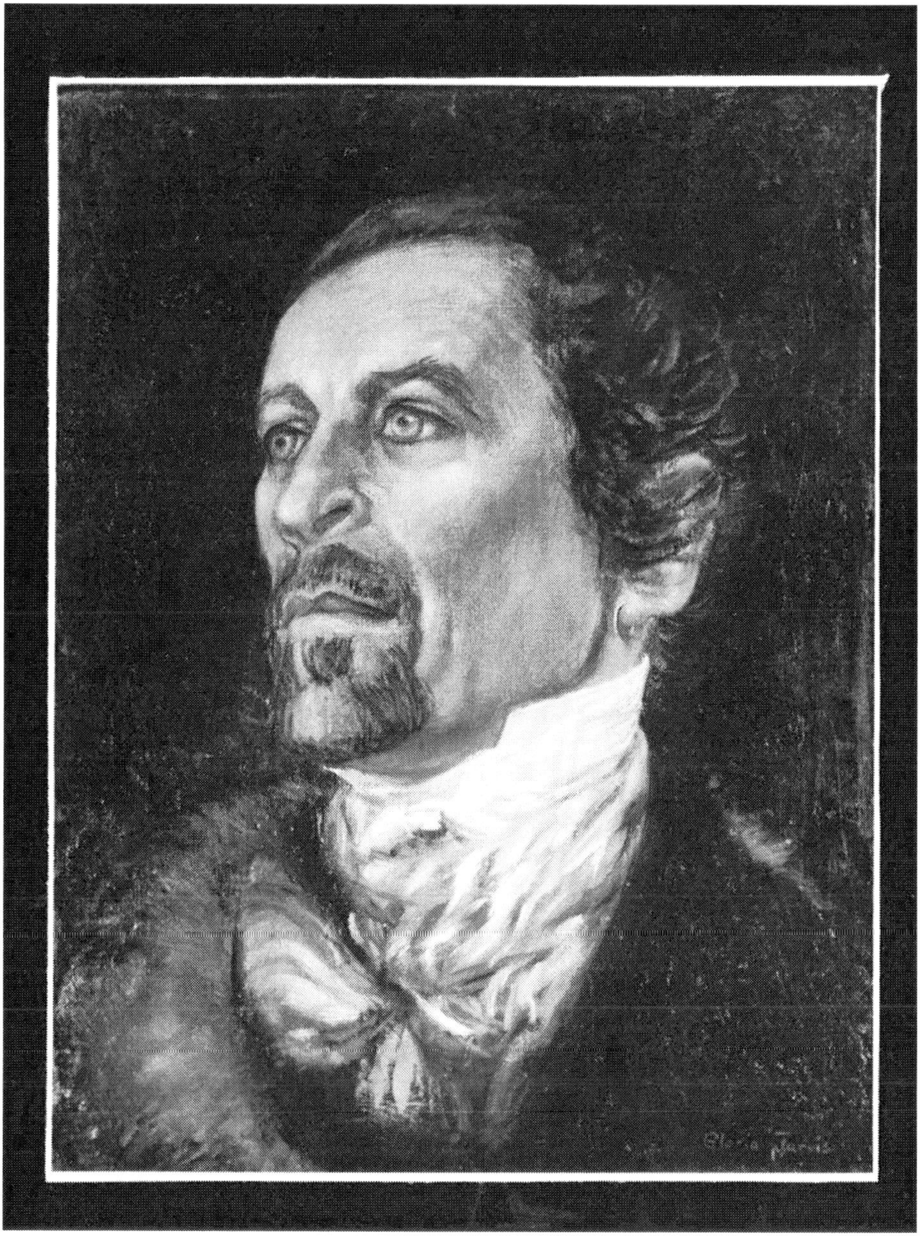

The dancer, Maurice Bejart - private collection
Portrait painted from sketches at rehearsal

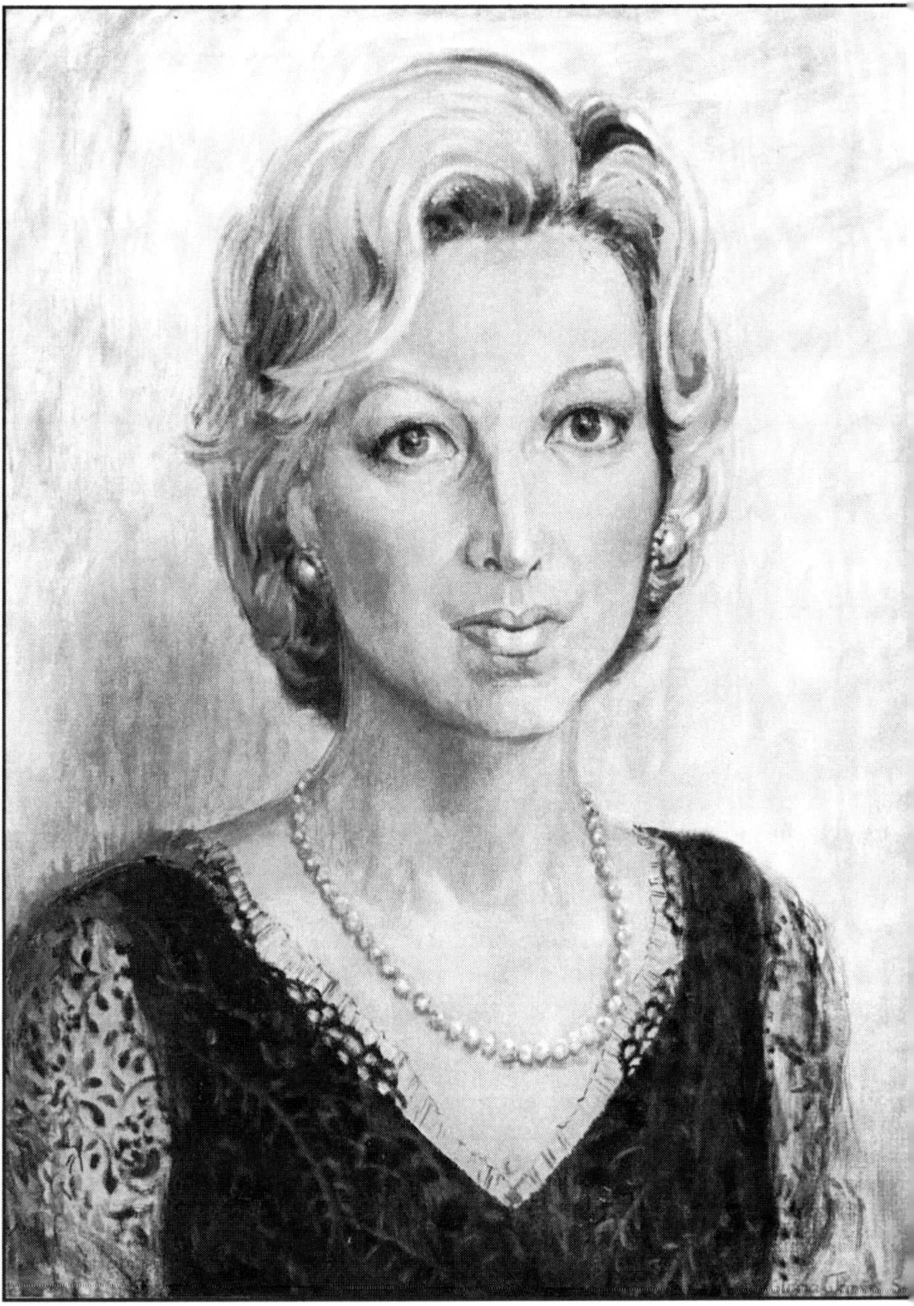

Madame Godon - private collection

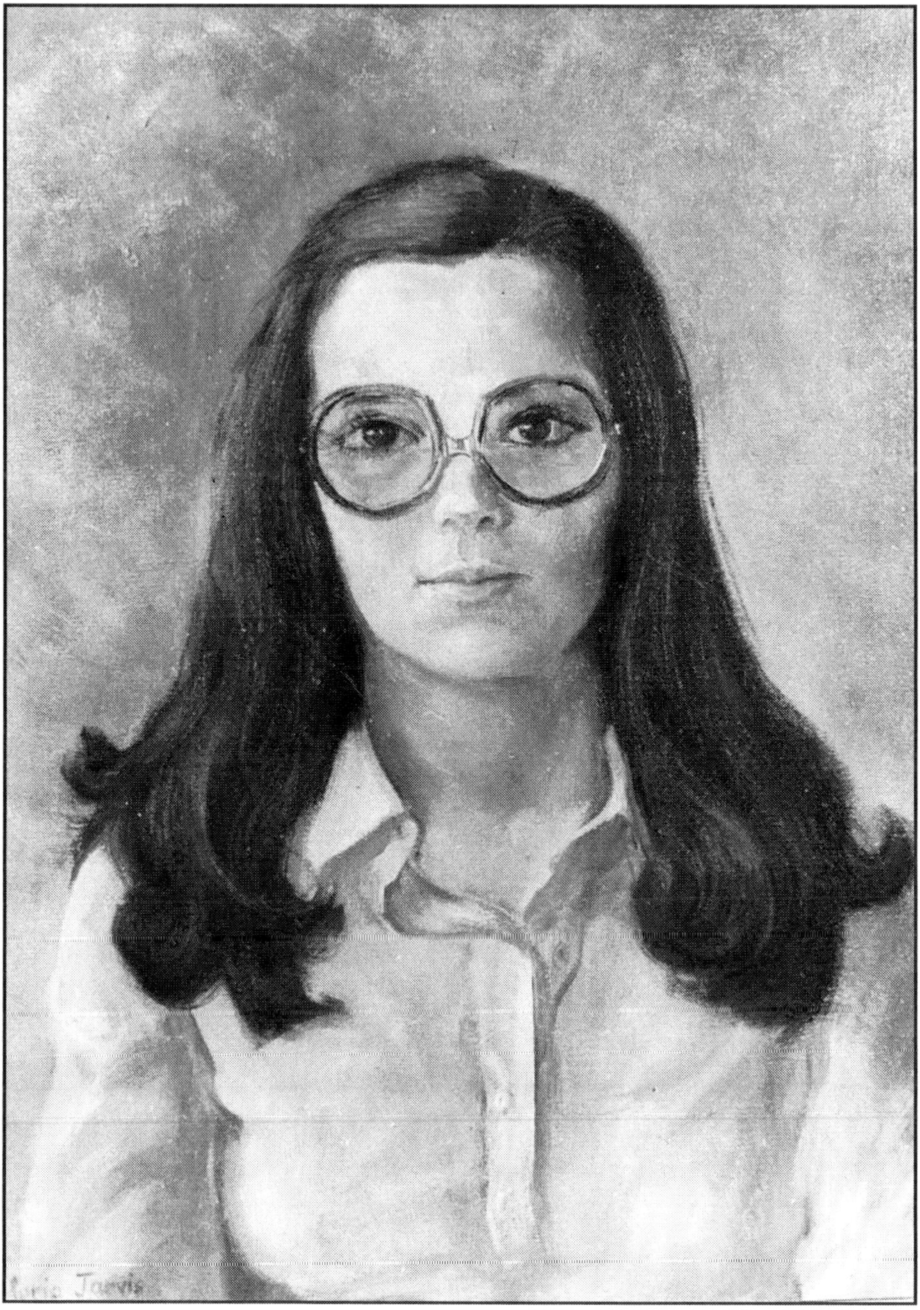

Portrait of Mademoiselle Maria di Fatima Perestrello
- private collection

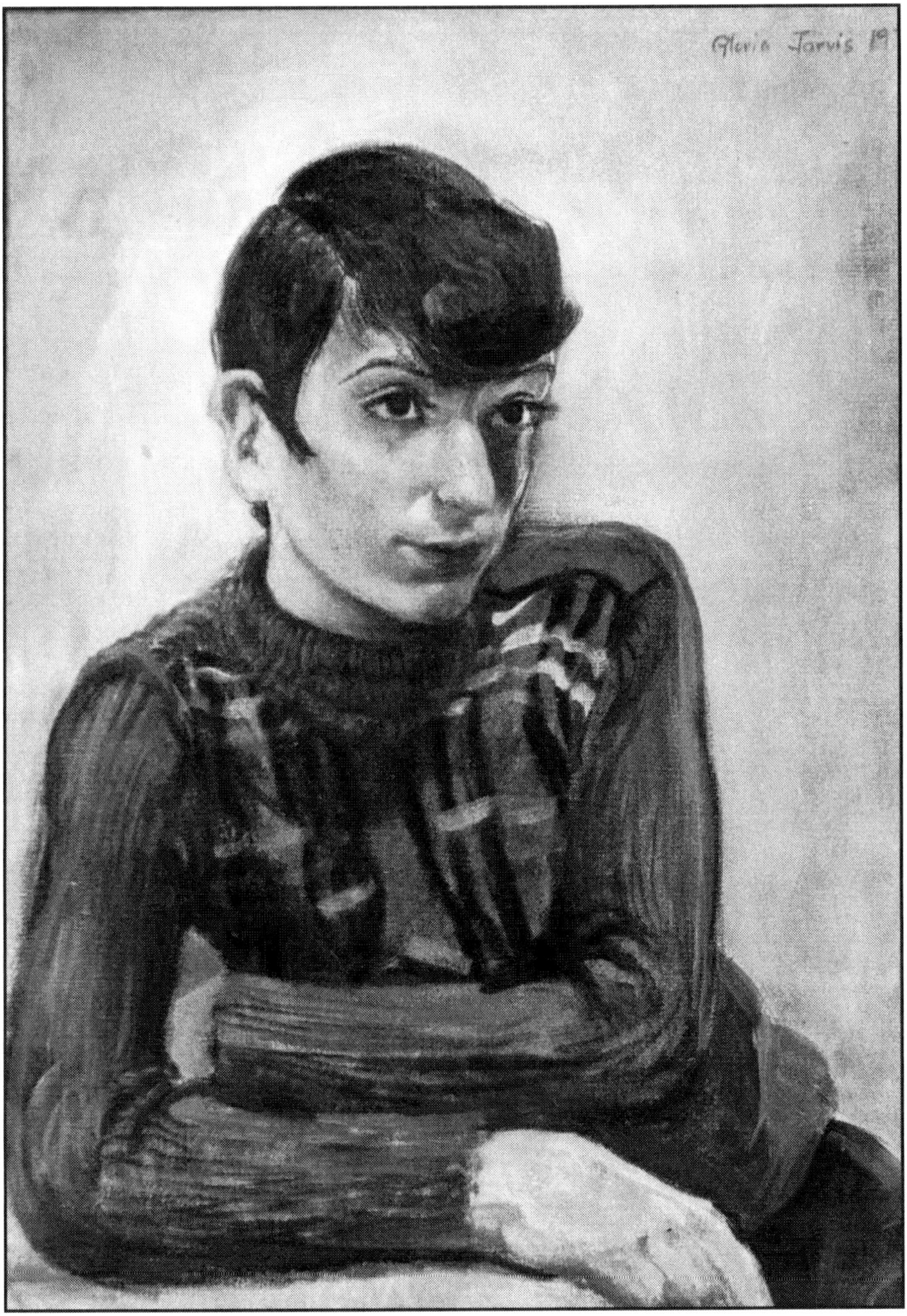

Portrait of Luciano - private collection

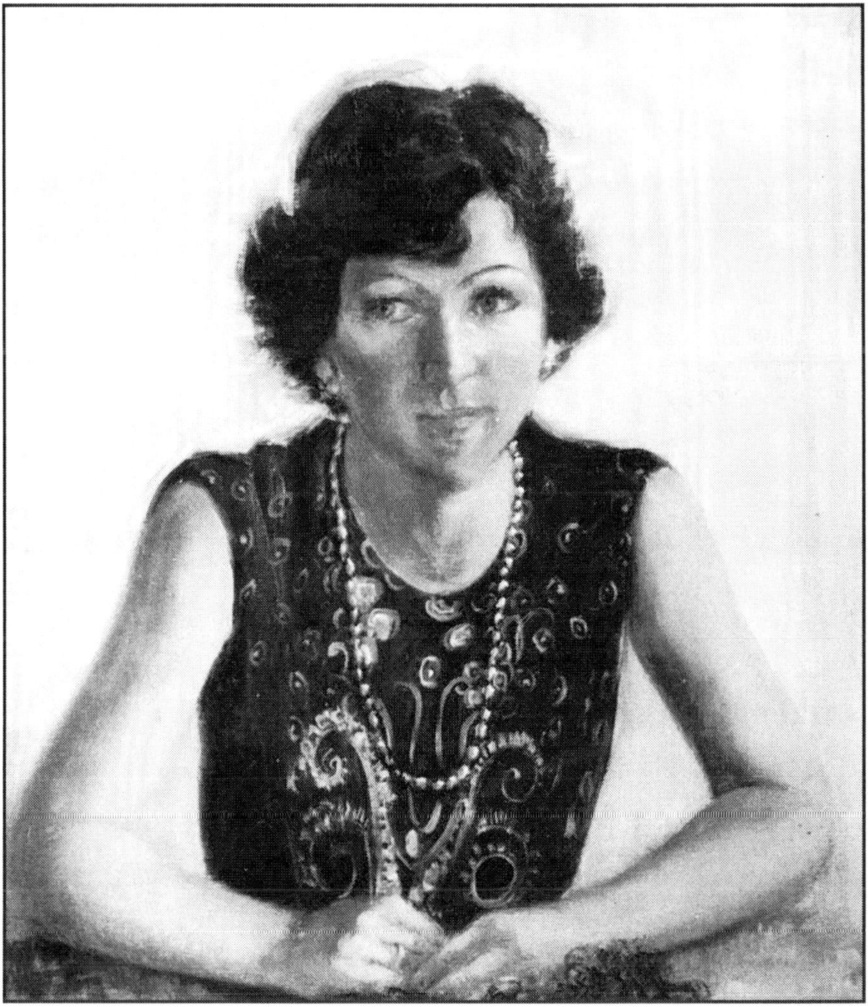

Portrait of a Lady - private collection

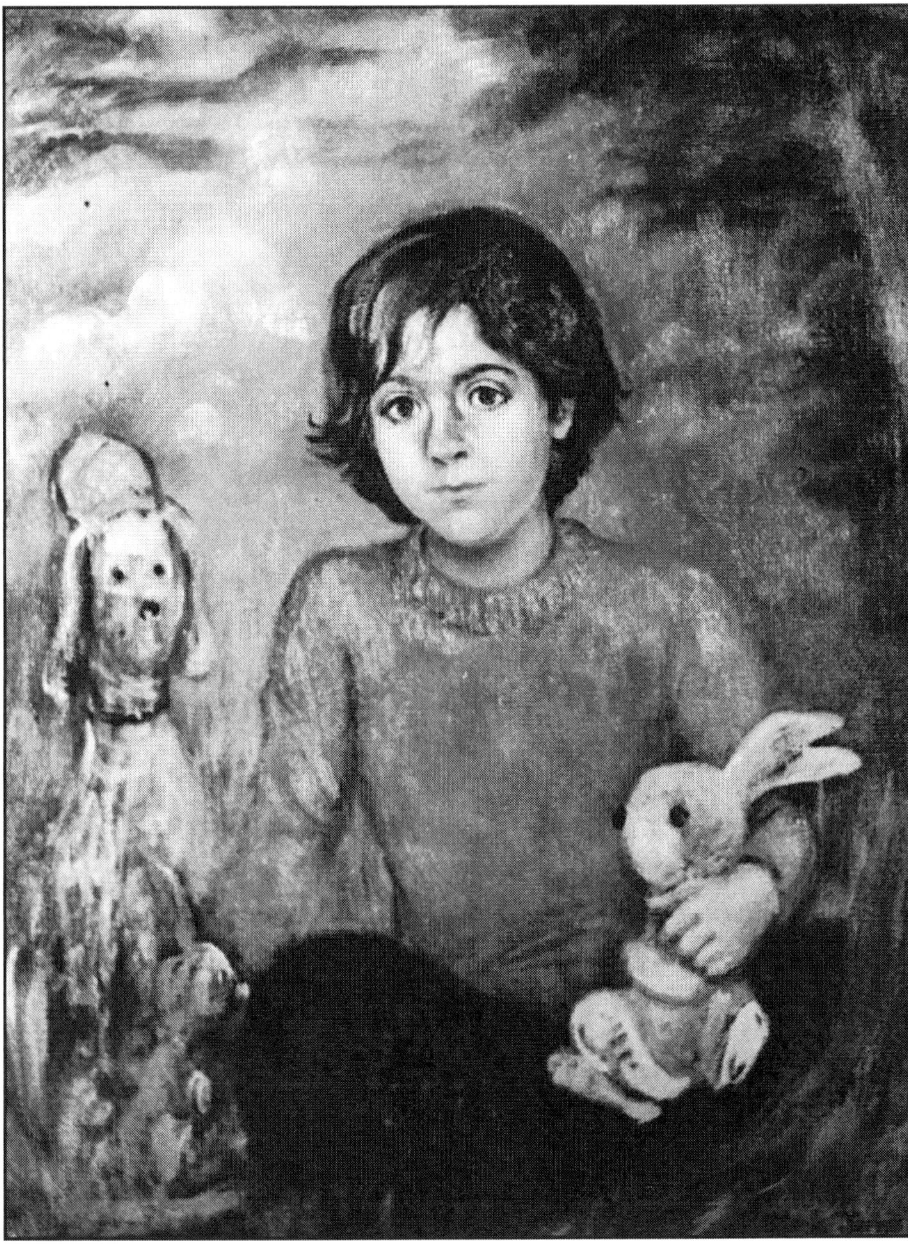

Portrait of Daniela - private collection

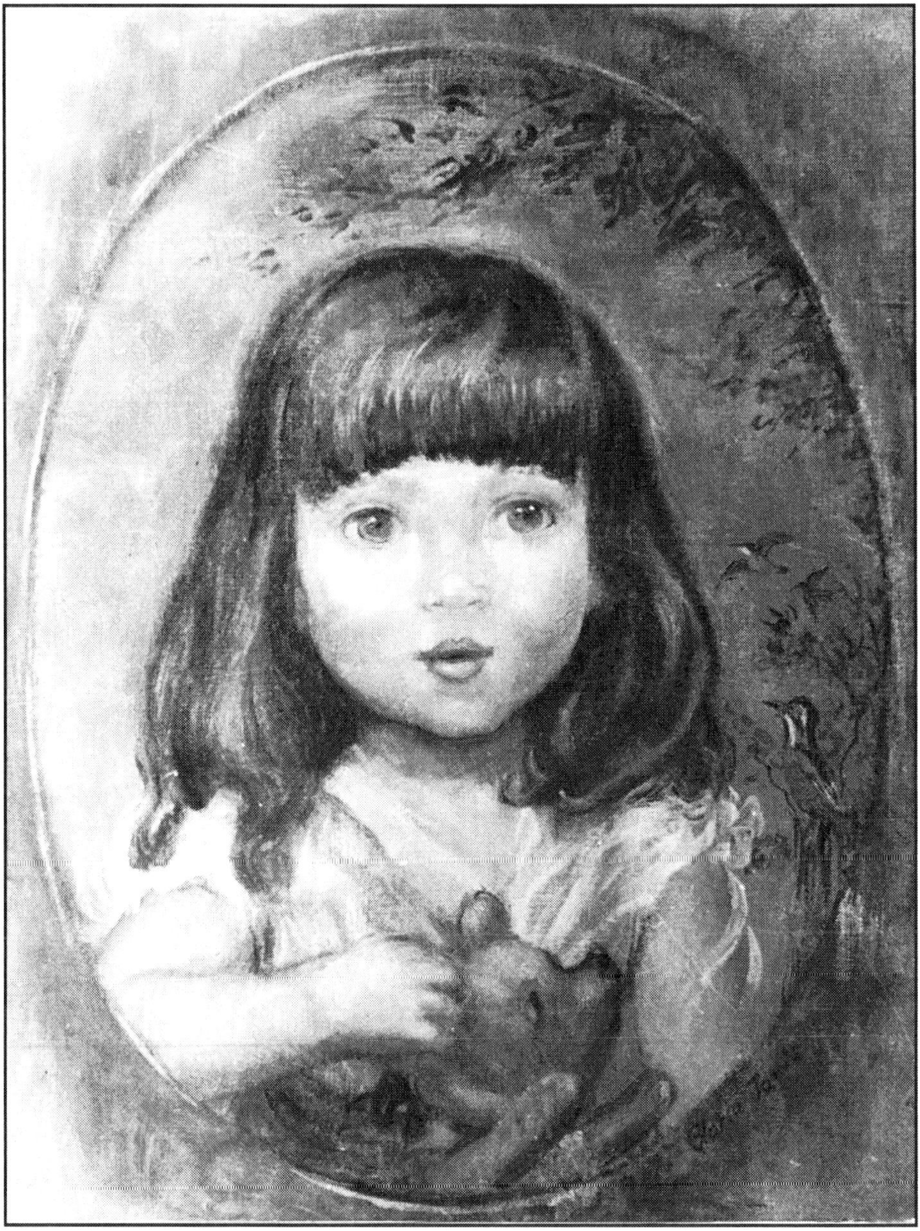

Portrait of a child - private collection

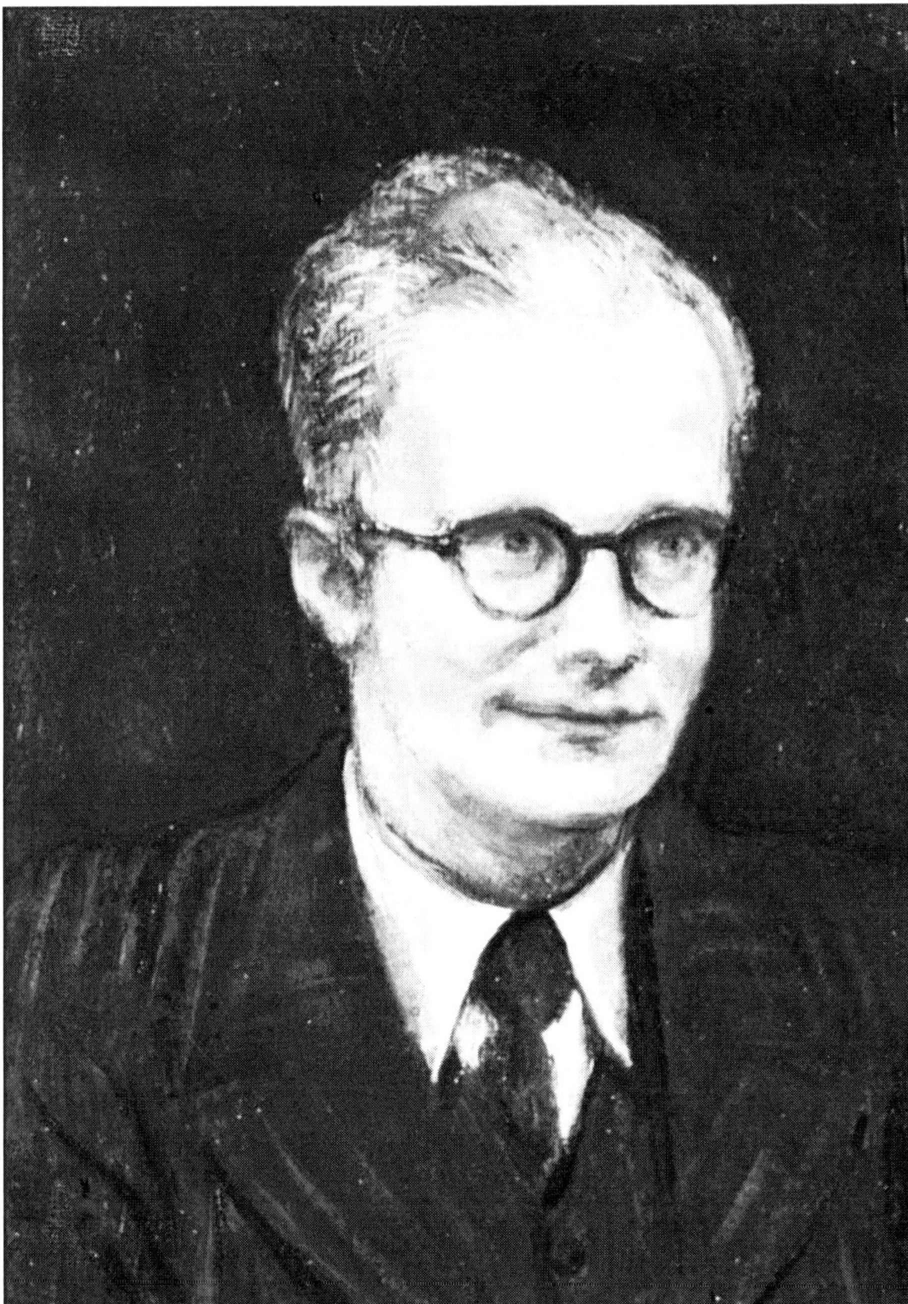

Monsieur Drabbé - posthumous portrait - private collection
Died in the Belgian Resistance

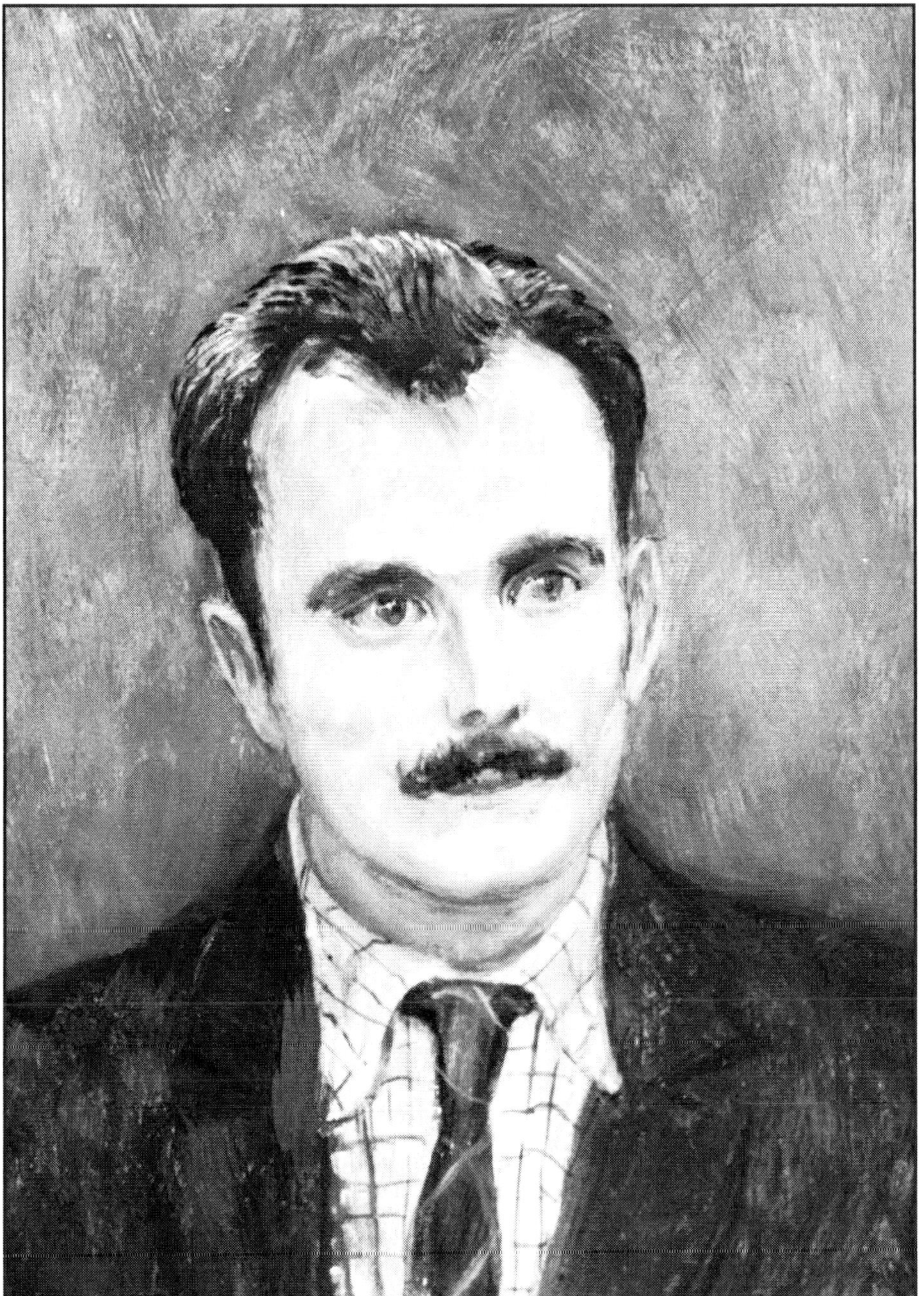

Monsieur Drabbé - posthumous portrait - private collection
Made up in disguise in the Belgian Resistance

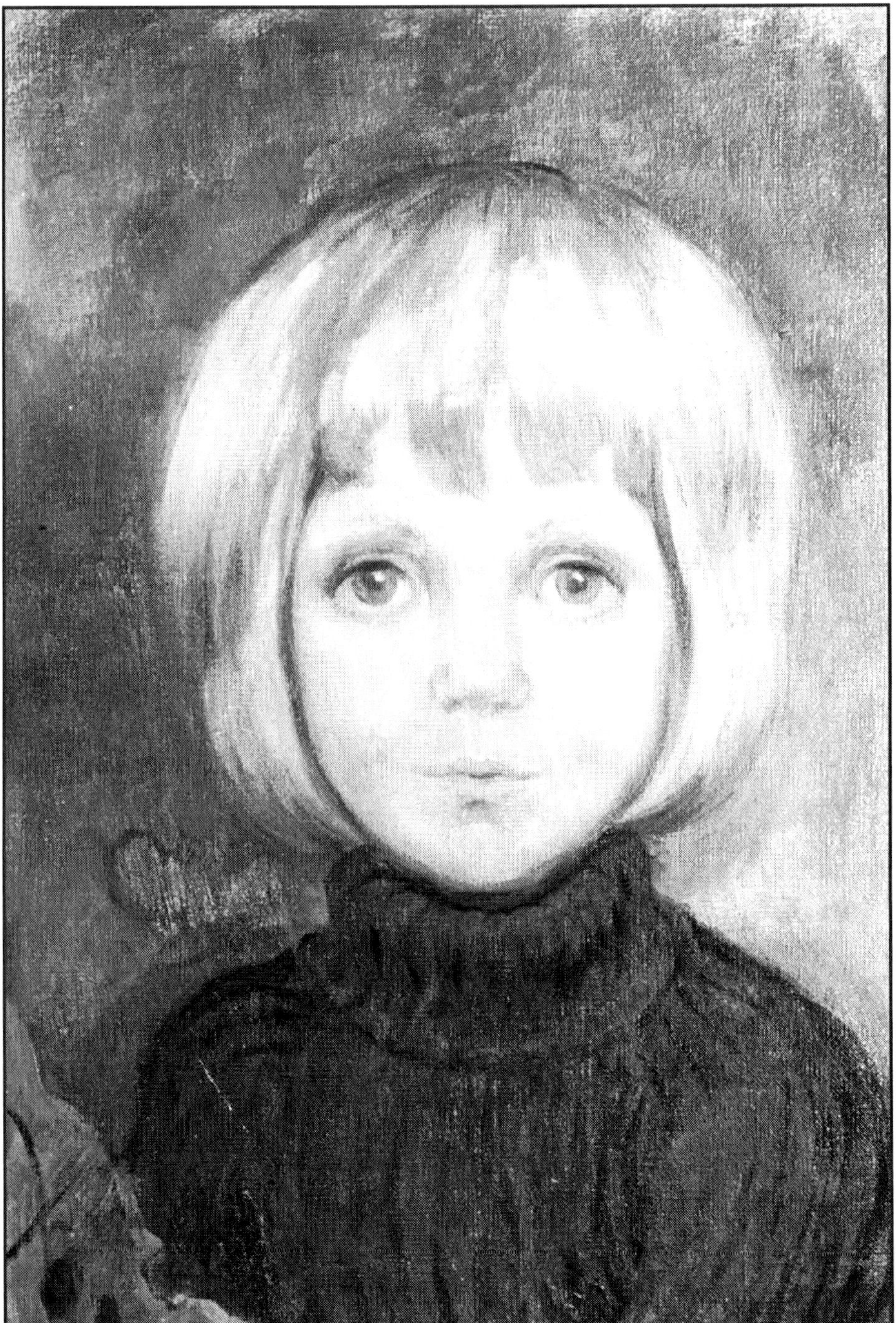

Daniela Kiesler - private collection

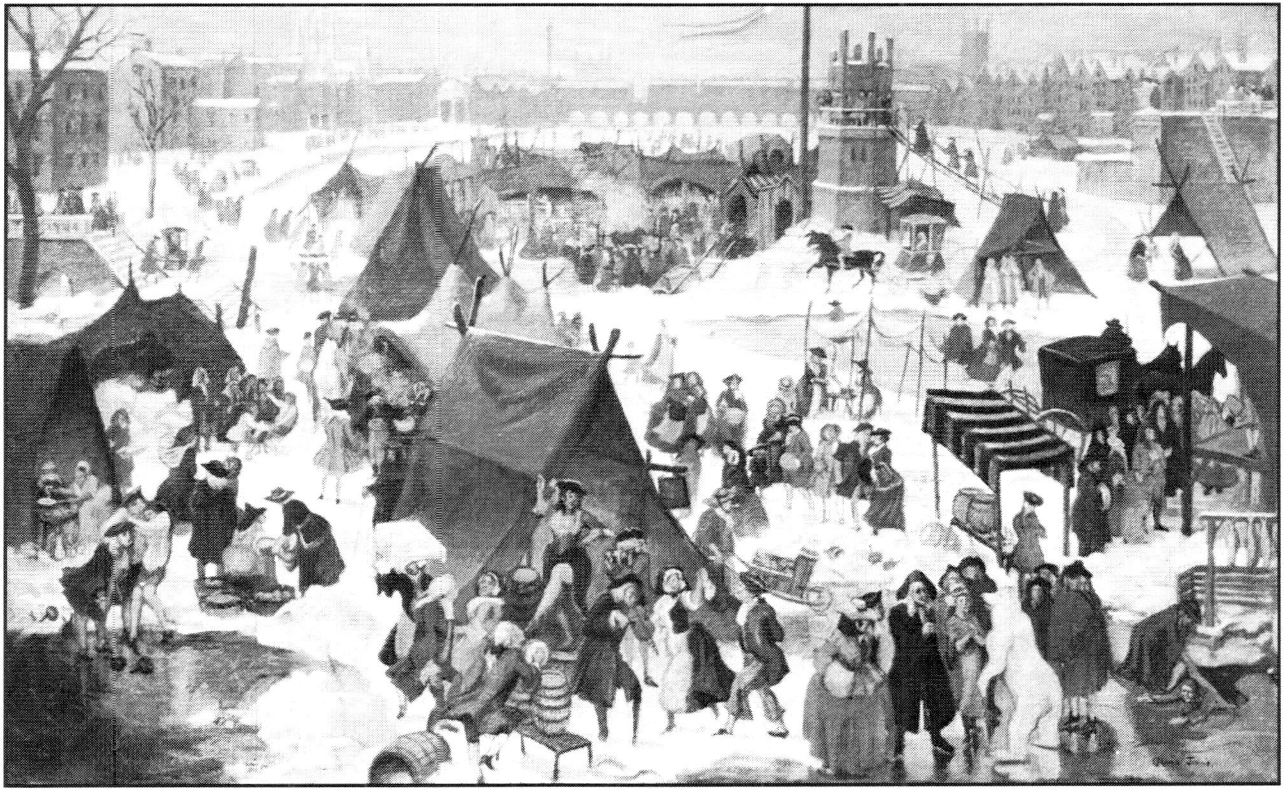

The Thames Frost Fair, 1740
The painting was formerly in the collection of Monsieur Charles Mouton, Brussels, and is at present in the collection of Dr De Grelle, Anderlues.

One day an elderly gentleman brought his granddaughter to Old England to be fitted for a party frock. While waiting he drew up one of the gilt chairs to contemplate my painting of the Thames Frost Fair, 1740; then decided he must have it for his collection, and – after a little haggling over price – bought it.

Realising that my painting had a sentimental value for me, and being a kindly soul, he said I would be welcome to come and see it again any time – an invitation I did take up. And what a wondrous occasion it was for me – for there it hung in his collection – proudly next to a Rubens portrait.

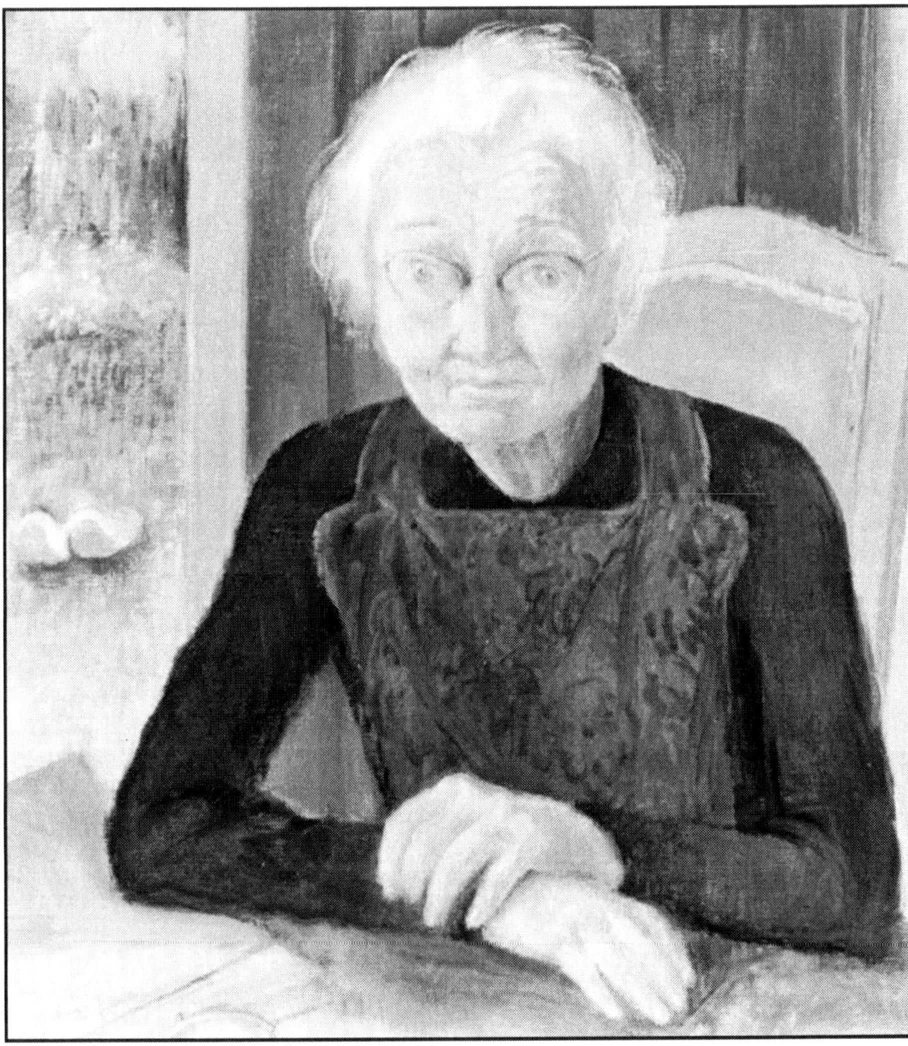

Oma (95 years old) - private collection

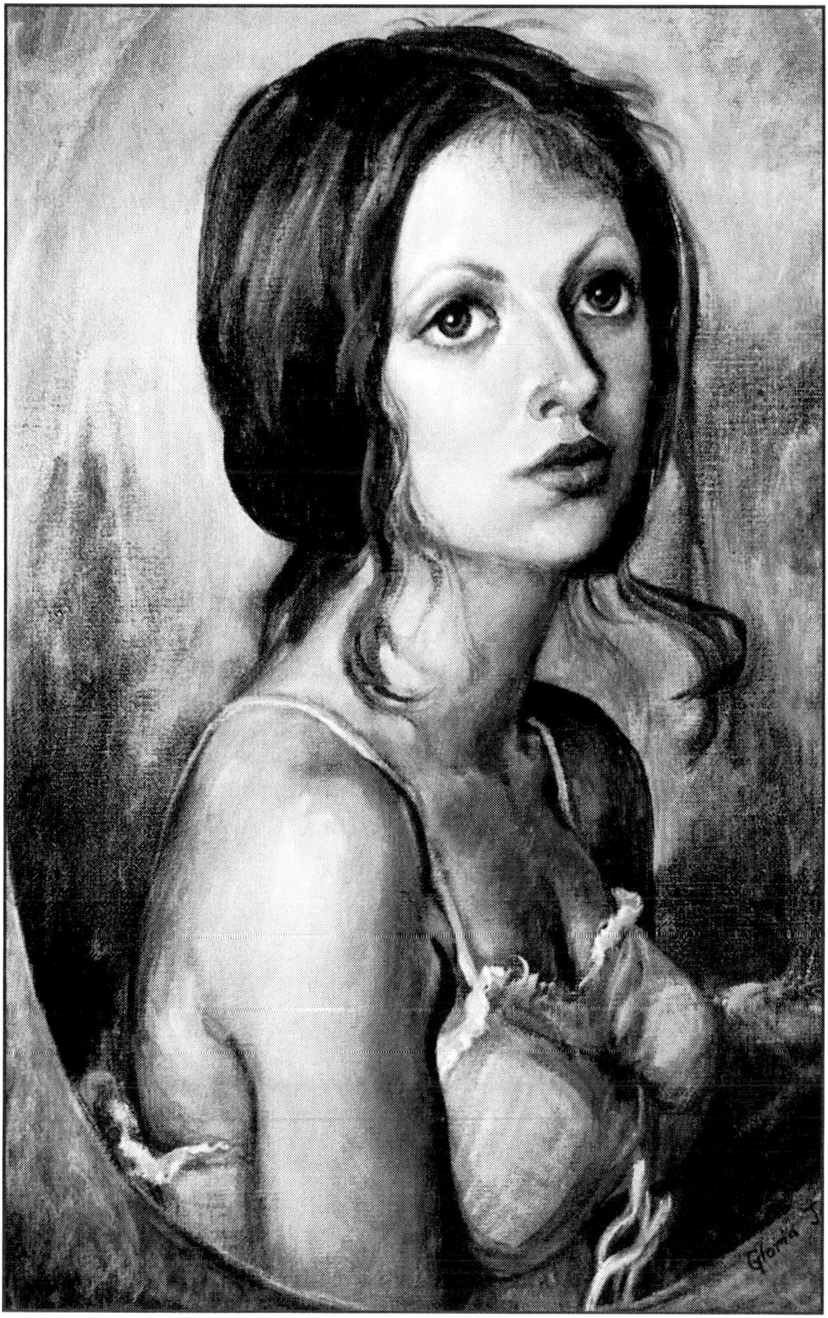

Portrait of Madame Biermé - private collection

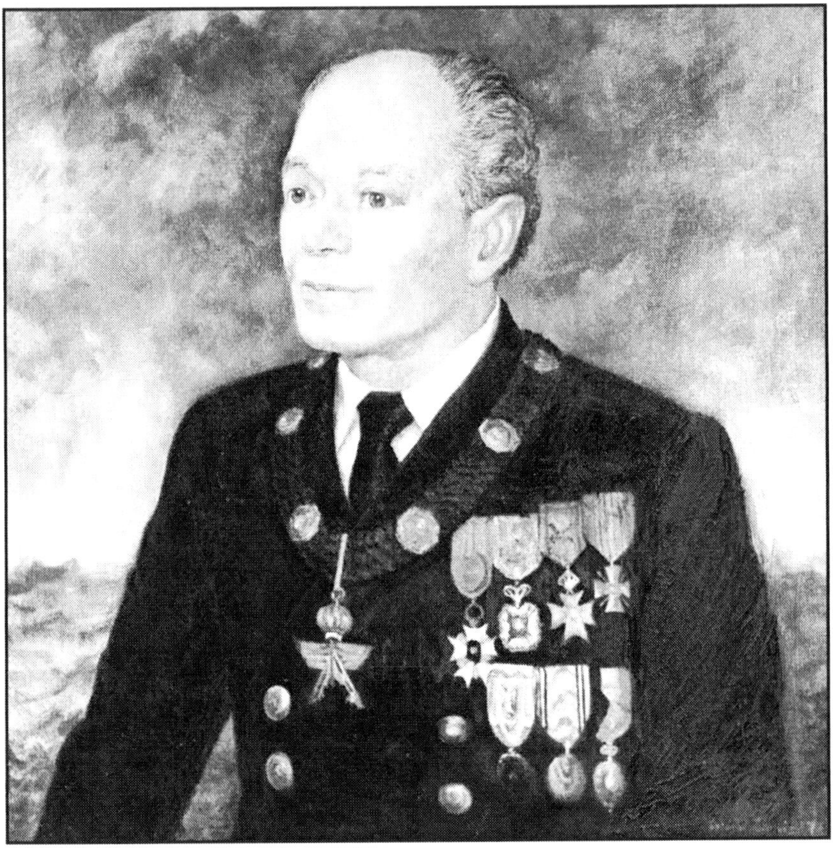

Le Commandant Albert Hubert - private collection

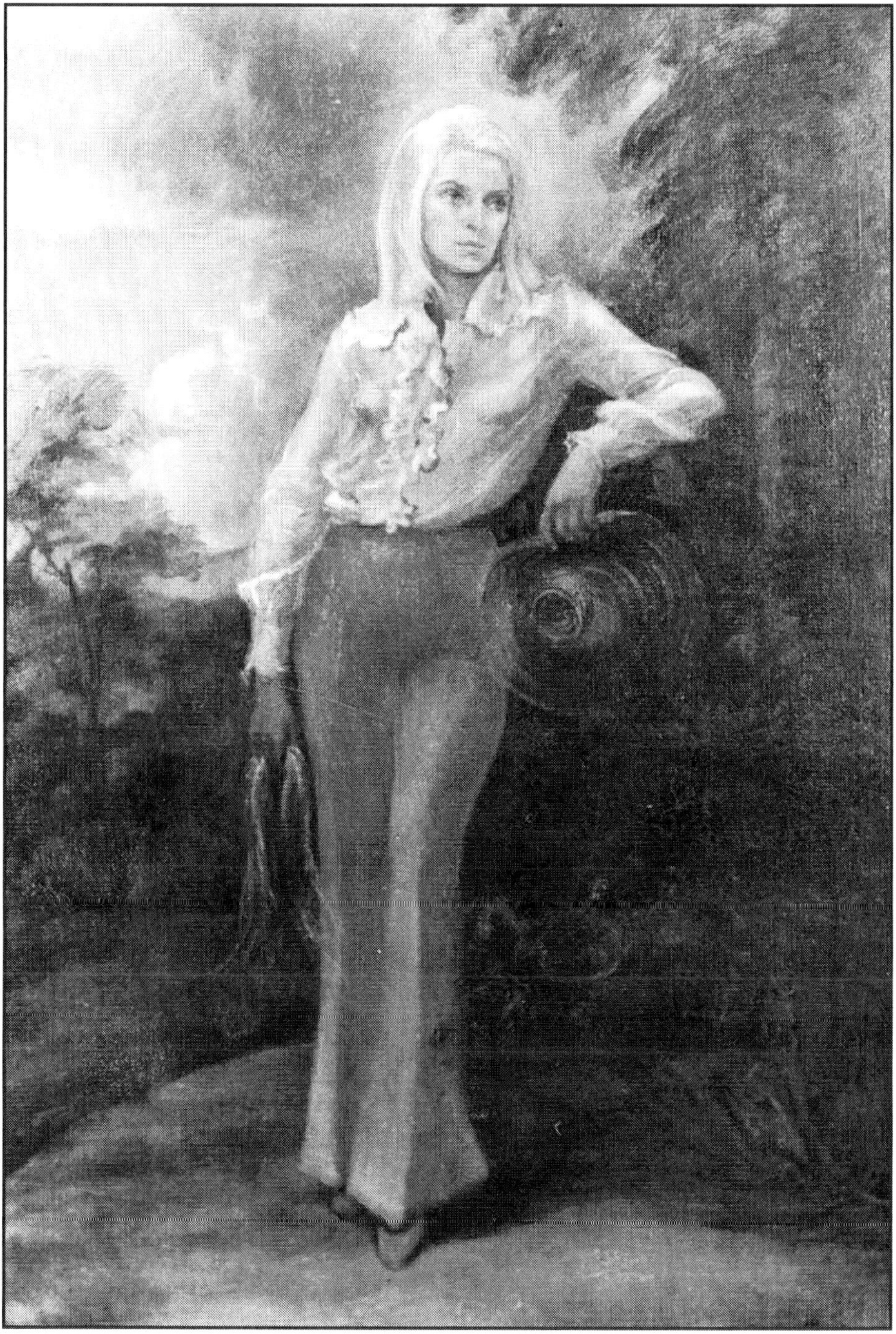

Portrait of Marie Badoux - private collection

4 THURSDAY, JUNE 26, 1975 Brussels Times

Ommegang replay is set for July 3 on Grand' Place

BY GLORIA SMITH

It was the dead of night and the city watch huddled over a wood fire. Soon, six chimes from the belfry of the Hôtel de Ville heralded daylight's beams into the square. The Grand'Place was suddenly invaded by gypsies whose boisterous gaiety galvanised the guard into a tour of the square. Then the Keeper of the Keys called on the Hôtel de Ville to open its gates, while from the adjacent streets the sixteenth-century Bruxellois in kermesse spirit sauntered onto the scene.

This is how it must have happened on that day in 1549, when Brussels honoured the visit of the Emperor Charles V and his sisters,

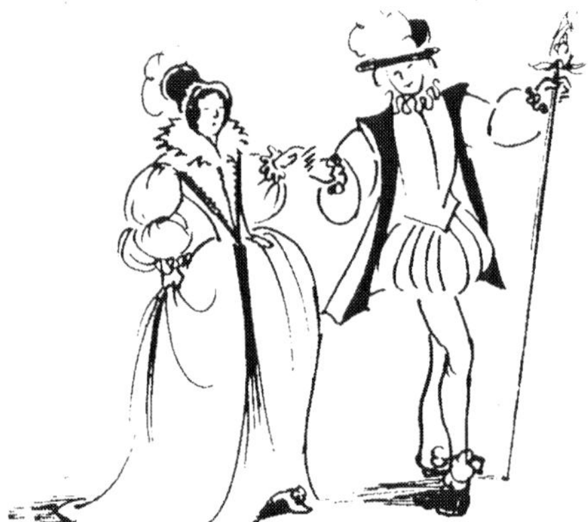

Eléanore of France and Marie of Hungary.

Trumpeters emerge from the Hôtel de Ville, face the belfry to give a fanfare. «Le Jeu de l'Ommegang» begins. This is Brussels' folkloric pageant, an evocation of the one given before Charles V, and now presented annually by the Société de l'Ommegang.

Ommegang is a Flemish word meaning «a going round». It was in 1927 that the founders of the Société de l'Ommegang revived the spectacle in its present form.

Its lay tradition originates from a religious legend which tells how, in 1348, Beatrix Soetkens, a poor draper's wife, was visited by the Virgin Mary in a dream. She was urged to go to Antwerp to find the miraculous little statue of «Our Lady of the Branch» and to transfer it to Brussels. There the statue was to be placed in the Chapel of the Sablon, which the Company of Crossbowmen had recently built—so the Virgin could acknowledge the good works of these crossbowmen for posterity. Béatrix went on her quest and successfully completed her mission. In fact, the archers themselves saw her skiff return haloed in light, accompanied by music. When the story was told, the City Fathers decreed that this sacred event should be commemorated each year by a procession. So, from the Legend of the Sablon, Ommegang was born.

There's nothing quite like it—and foreigners love it as much as the Belgians, as proved by the Ommegang success in Munich and in Canada for Expo 67. Tourists also flock to Brussels to see it.

An old painting comes to life as the procession of the City Elders builds up to the grand entry of the Royals—Charles V, Eléanore of France and Marie of Hungary, and their respective courts—all represented by Belgium's ancient and noble families, who administer the Société de l'Ommegang.

They also go on a stately progress round and round before coming to rest on the dais in front of the Maison du Roi, where they view the ensuing contests.

They and other revellers thrill to the joie-de-vivre of the folkdancers, the wizardry of the flag bearers in «Le Jeu des Drapeaux» with its race, and the incomparable stilt-walkers in tourney—stilts were practical gear in the past to get over the marshy countryside of Brabant. The floats bearing the Legend of the Sablon and the Legend of St Gudule go past, as do the Knights of the Noble Order of the Golden Fleece; then the beautiful Pucelle of Brussels appears, sitting under a golden canopy. She releases a flight of doves as a sign of Peace and the effect is breathtaking.

My article for the Brussels Times

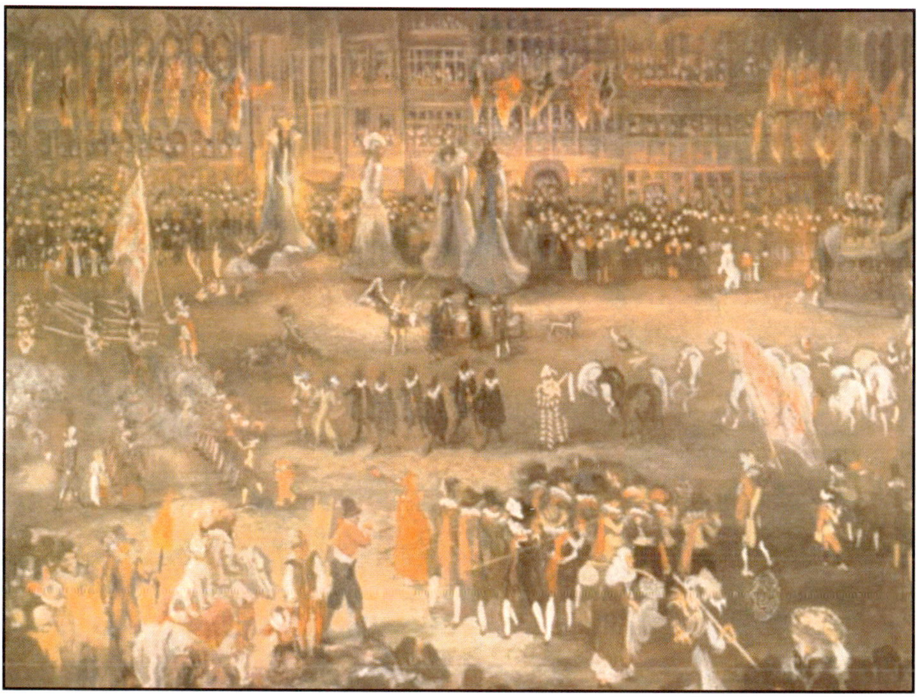

"Ommegang" meaning "a going round" held on several summer evenings a year - together with my article for the Brussels Times. As with all my historical reconstructions the composition is entirely original

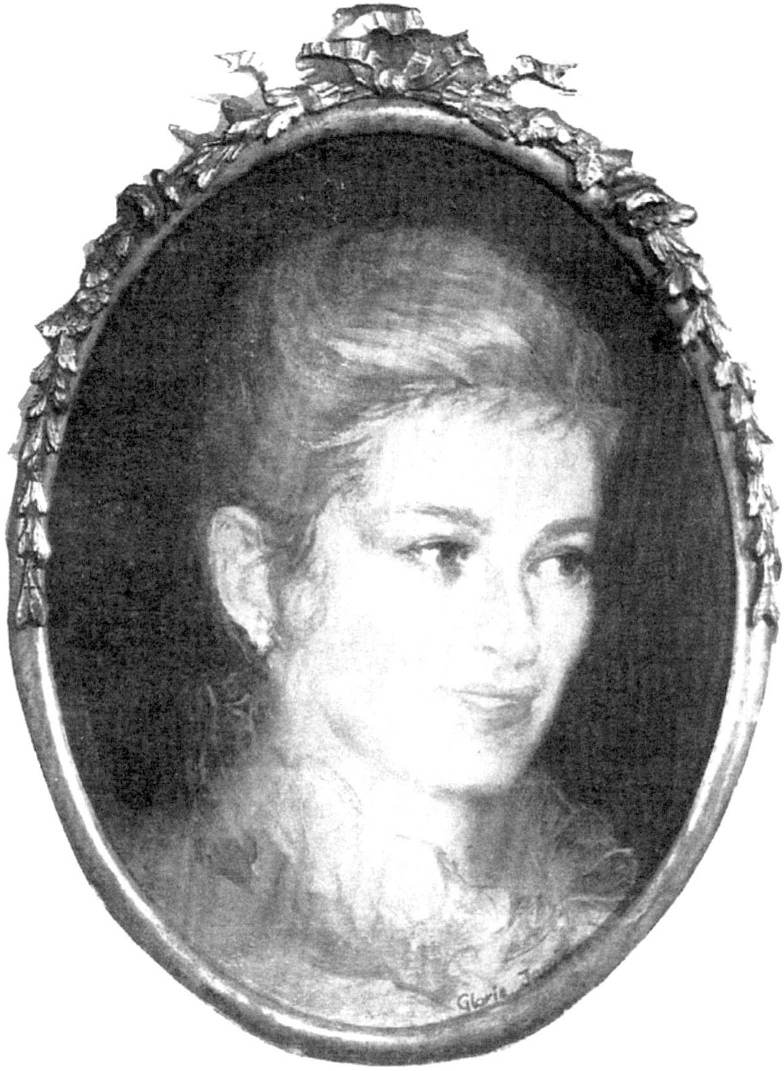

Sa Altesse Royale Princess of Liège, now Queen of the Belgians

The Palace of Belvedere

"Ah, but I was younger then!" said the Princess wistfully, gazing down at her youthful face of years ago.

We were standing in the centre of the domed rotunda in her classical palace at Laeken, a few miles from Brussels. I had just that moment drawn back the tissue paper covering the portrait I had painted of her, now cradled in the crook of my arm, and which I was on the point of presenting to her. It was to be a parting gesture before leaving Belgium – which I had come to regard affectionately as my second country. A Belgian friend had told me etiquette precluded anyone setting eyes on it before the royal recipient herself – Paola, Princess of Liège.

"Are you Madame Gloria Jarvis?" had asked the gendarme through my taxi window at the entrance to Belvedere. And after phoning the Palace of my arrival we swept up the drive.

To cross the classical threshold was to savour a new environment. Ushered into a small ante waiting room, I had time to contemplate my introductory speech in French which in 16 years had become quite fluent – in contrast to nowadays.

The equerry appeared in naval uniform (seeing he was captain of a frigate) and led me up a flowing staircase to the rotunda. There in its midst stood the Princess Paola (who has since changed residence for the Royal Palace of Brussels after she and her husband ascended the throne).

When years later I remembered her charming reception of me it moved me to turn it into a poem. Entitled: "Close Encounter" it perhaps will give the feel of the occasion if included here:

12.5.78
"L'Eventail"

WHO'S WHO IN ART PAINTS WHO'S WHO

Gloria Jarvis has a delightful way of seeing Brussels as it was and will, alas, not be again. The pitures she paints of eighteenth century comedians in the *Grand'Place*, a pre-neon *Place de Brouckere* and a wonderful *Ommegang* in full regalia show her love of history and that flair for drama one would expect in someone who has studied and worked at stage design. Her affinity for Breughelian scenes was already apparent in herj 1952 *Frost Fair*, a wide sweep of icy events during the great freeze of 1750 when Londoners took their revels right out onto the frozen Thames.

But love of historical settings doesn't blind her to the charms of life in today's city. She and her English husband have loved living in Brussels these past ten years and have lots of Belgian friends. She sees some of them at crack - of - dawn weekend expeditions with the Cercle de Pegase, her walking group, which is headed for Basel this spring. When asked what sort of people belonged to Pegase, she said, « oh, they come from all walks of life ».

Shakespeare would have loved Gloria Jarvis' « ever soft, gentle and low » voice. Perhaps its excellent quality owes something to the deep sense of contentment in which she seems to move. She's had plenty of recognition : including the *Medaille d'Argent* from *Arts, Sciences, Lettres*, Paris, is listed in Who's Who in Art and the World Who's Who of Women, and was graduated brilliantly from St. Martin's School of Art in London. Her career has included posts as professor of design in the history of costume, being assistant to Royal Academician James Bateman, doing illustrations for Macmillan and murals on the walls of the English school of Florence, where she says she spent « the most wonderful period of my life » studying with the great Robert Longhi there. When Old England was in the Place Royal, she had a studio there and numerous exhibitions.

It is clear she loves to paint and that pleasure transfers itself to the viewer of her pictures. She can and does paint in lots of different ways ranging from serious portraits to wittily-observed courtroom scenes at Old Bailey. The portraits she considers most exacting, having to walk that tightrope of pleasing the sitter, while remaining honest to herself.

It's a pity Bejart hasn't seen the rivetting one she's done of him from photographs : it exactly catches his Mephistophalian charm. A small head of Princess Paola is the very image of her sweet wistfulness. Gloria Jarvis loves to paint children and often shows them in romantic hats. Hats again figure in a dandified group of Harrow boys in their summer boaters. She can as easily switch to a deeper level as in the touching scene she did of an aged Churchill visiting his alma mater.

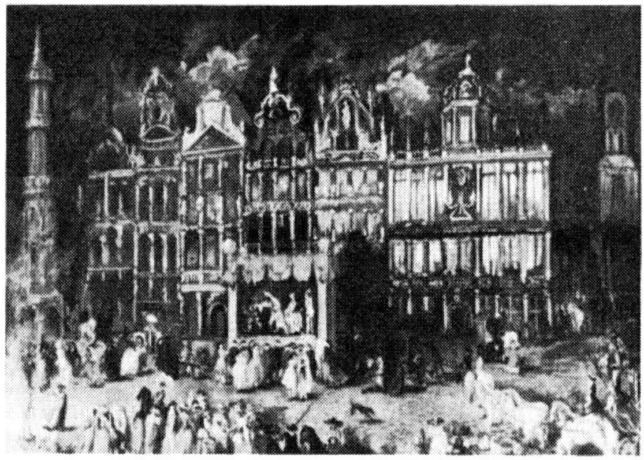

Italian Comedians play in the Grand'Place (2nd half 18th C.).

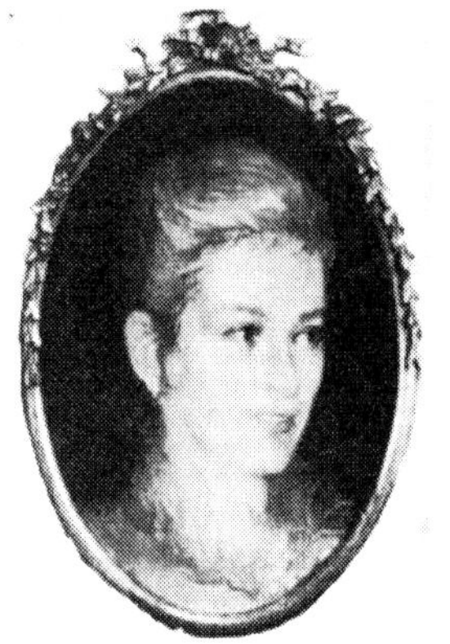

S.A.R. the Princess of Liege.

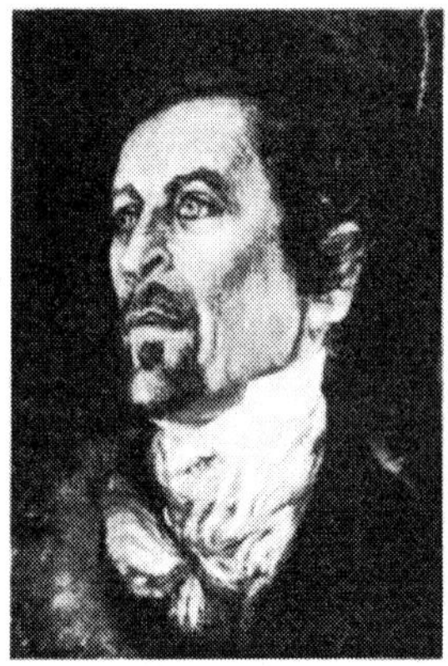

Maurice Bejart.

She enriched her palette and her powers of observation after graduation, when she and a group of artists teamed up in a Soho studio. They invited people in off the street to pose. Besides sharpening their eyes, they experimented in different media. And today, she's as versatile in oil as in gouache and pastels. She enjoys the discipline of gouache on tinted paper, where the artist tries (and succeeds in her case) to tell the story putting in as little as possible.

And that's not all. Lately she has tried another form of communication — writing. Gloria Jarvis started writing in 1970 for the British Beacon and the late, lamented Brussels Times. She's done some short stories that have been read on the BBC and she would like to do more.

When you look at her pictures with their loving observation of the past, it comes as no surprise that she is not much for abstract art, though she has painted one abstract that has been accepted by the Royal Academy in London. But she feels, « it's so difficult to represent life on a flat surface », she prefers to stay with that, because for her « life is everything ». She doesn't like the cult of ugliness and she says she doesn't care « two hoots » if people say she's reactionary. She knows her pictures strike a chord in plenty of people, because they constantly tell her so at all her exhibitions — she's had six so far in Belgium, and is working on a spring one for Etterbeek.

She can only express what she feels, she says. What appeals about the past is how people tried to express beauty. She has, she feels, stayed true to her original concept of style and the only thing that's changed is that now she's surer of herself, and the work goes faster.

S.W.

Close Encounter

I had a close encounter with a queen.
She was a princess then – it's now she reigns.
Her gown was long and black, light ashen blond her hair –
Sylph-like and boyish, extending a pale hand in polite greeting,
A lovely centre-piece in that glass-domed rotunda.
A sheet of tissue paper loosely covering the portrait I had painted of her,
Once removed, revealed that royal image fair of sixteen years ago.
Her Royal Highness smiled a wistful smile:
"Ah, yes," she said "I was much younger, then!"...
Ordered a flunkey to bring coffee,
Motioned to a couch of Louis Seize,
And set the oval frame upon a rosewood table.
Coffee was served, the flunkey all a-gleam in pristine gloves –
As we sat chatting, she and I, an interview simplicity itself...
Until I'd stayed as long as etiquette permitted.
Both rose and sauntered to the door, exchanged adieus –
She thanking me most warmly for my gift.
This gesture on my part would mark my quitting Belgium
With nigh on sixteen years of ex-pat. residence,
When many portraits issued from my brush
Through having done this lady's – which stood guarantor
Of my ability to capture a true likeness.
Now, grateful for commissions that her lovely image brought me,
This portrait I surrendered to its source of inspiration.

The princess sent me home in one of the royal cars.
Half an hour before I had left my Brussels flat just off Avenue de Tervuren in a mere taxi. Calling out my destination with its important ring: "The Palace of Belvedere", I heard the unwitting reply:
"Do you mean the pub?"

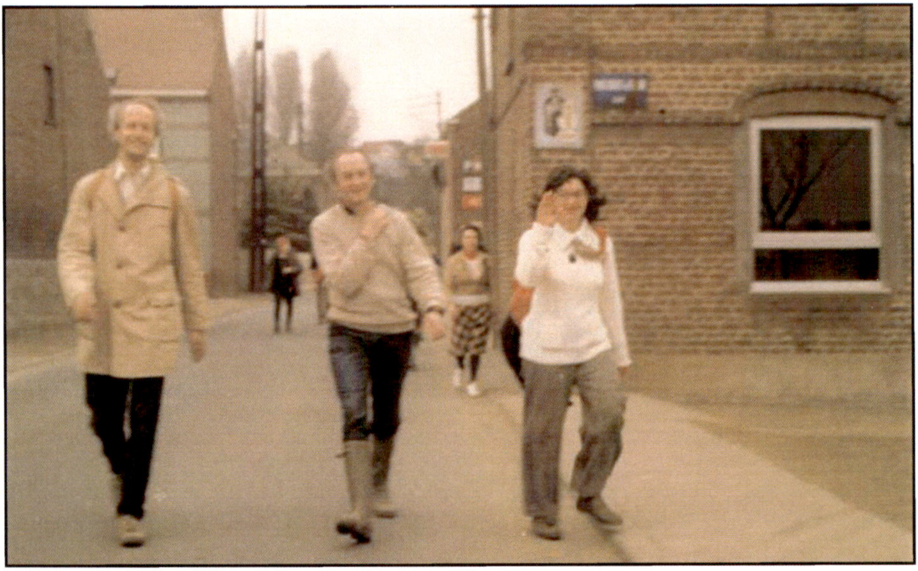

Marathon March 1978 - myself with Henryk and Dirk, two Danes

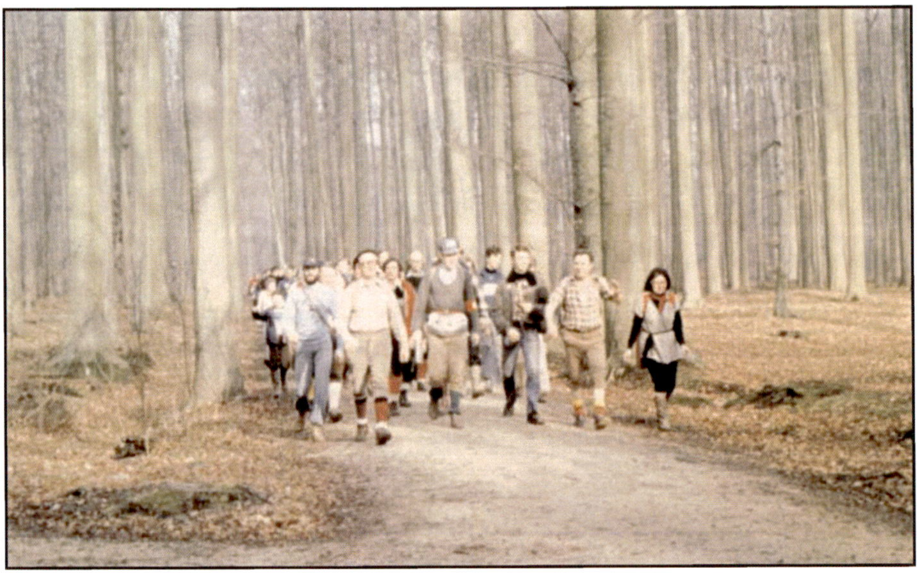

A Pégase marathon through the Forêt de Soignes (myself far right)

Wing-footed Pégase

A walking group with the name of Pégase has to be fleet of foot. As a member that is what I became, with the joy of seeing Belgium in its entirety, as well as meeting a good cross section of its population. Besides, being the only Englishwoman among them gave me a rarity value that caused much bonhomie between us. They came to the private views of my exhibitions and were kind enough to buy some of my work, thus becoming patrons.

Every Sunday at crack of dawn we would assemble at one of the main line stations to board either train or coach to take us to one of the country's various scenic regions, joined on the way by others, like the stalwart Jean de Namur, as he was known.

I shall remember always the mist of a winter's morning through the trees of some forest in the province of Luxembourg; picnics in snowy February in the Fagnes, where I almost disappeared down a hole in the undergrowth of the bog-infested ground if the strong man behind had not caught me and pulled me back; and the café whose rear end doubled as a funeral parlour and where we overflowed to eat our sandwiches at the long table fit for a corpse; nearby an old upright piano had its sheet of music open at a hymn. Coffins of all sizes – interiors in a choice of fabrics – lined the way to the toilets, which should have made us reflect on our own mortality. But the lugubriousness of it all had its funny side.

The friendly atmosphere engendered by a twenty kilometre walk culminated in the "verre d'amitié" imbibed in a café before the trek back to Brussels when the homeward journey by coach or train was a very merry one indeed!

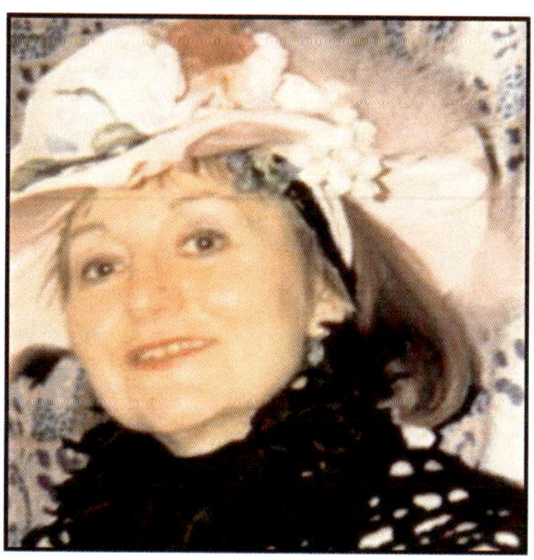

Myself at the Pégase fancy dress ball

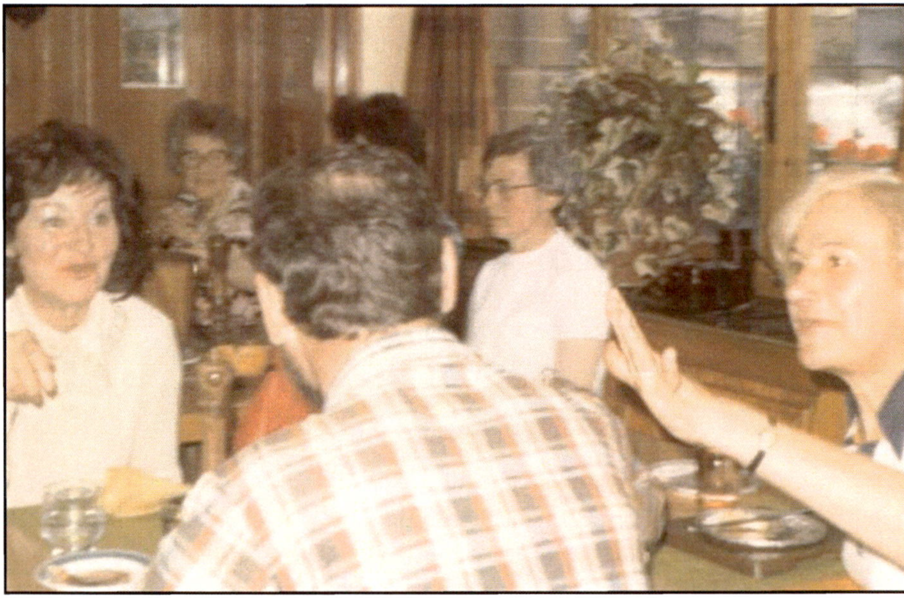

A trek ends in Basle with the Swiss speciality: La Raclette (myself on left)

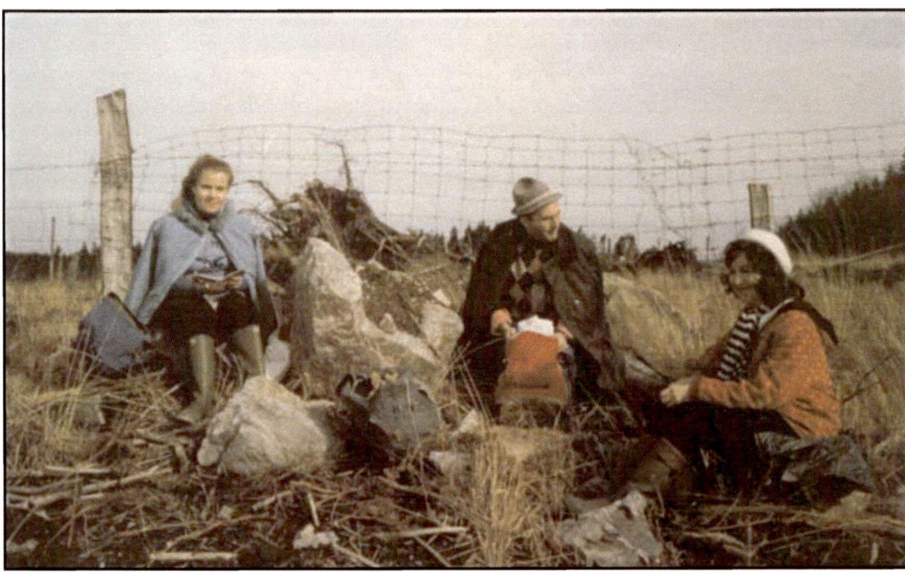

Part of a February picnic. Three walkers of Pégase (myself on right), in the Fagnes countryside.

Aftermath

Had once a bloody battle passed that way?
Did sudden ambush break the noonday calm
Of German soldiers resting in the hay,
Mid alien country, on a Belgian farm?
In tangled grass a Nazi's helmet lay -
Kicked as I skirted round that self-same field -
But rusty after fifty years' decay,
Reminder of a soldier's fate long sealed.
I picked it up to contemplate my find.
I said 'Poor Yorick! See how small a head' -
Merely a lad, his adolescent mind
Uncomprehending as he joined the dead.

No epitaph in stone could quite surpass
This hemet - poignant relic in the grass.

Written years after this hauting experience.

Home and Genealogy

Eventually it was a return home to care for my parents back in England. Following their demise within five months of one another I decided to trace my family history, given a lead years ago by my paternal grandfather, when I had questioned him in my youth. After a long period of research I found I had gathered enough material for the publication of two books, one Tudor to Victorian, the other covering the twentieth century till recent times.

Ah memory, precious memory… for without grandfather casting his mind back to a Victorian childhood my family tree might not have got off the ground, and his own lovable grandfather would have remained in obscurity, leaving me the poorer.

Gradually there emerged a cavalcade of Buckinghamshire yeomen farming their freehold acres of arable and pasture around the village of Haddenham, south-west of Aylesbury, almost into Oxfordshire. I got to know them through their Wills – so much so, that if I were to meet them one day – it would be just like greeting old friends. The earliest Will dates from 1557.

As for the next book – they would float across my imagination – those individuals from whom I had the good fortune to hear at first hand the personal memories of all those Jarvis relatives who lit up the family scene throughout a large part of the twentieth century.

Writing has now taken over as a creative force and supplanted painting in that sphere; it has become my "raison d'être". But the fact of having to choose between writing and art as a career suggests I can claim both as part of my life's work, since changing eyesight has forced me to abandon the easel.

A JARVIS TAPESTRY
Gloria Jarvis Smith
£5.99, plus £2.00 p&p from Gloria Jarvis Smith, The Bungalow, Tyler Close, Canterbury, Kent CT2 7BD. It is also available in museums and local studies centres in Buckinghamshire as well as at Aylesbury County Library.
This book traces the story of the Jarvises, a Buckinghamshire family, from Tudor to Victorian times. Interwoven with the social history of the times in which they lived and beautifully illustrated by the author, who is a talented artist as well as a writer, it goes far beyond the history of one family and has universal appeal.

THE HISTORICAL NOVELS REVIEW

ISSUE 25, AUG 2003

A Jarvis Tapestry
The Early History of a Buckinghamshire Family from Tudor to Victorian Times
by Gloria Jarvis Smith Published by the author, 2003. The Bungalow, Tyler Close, Canterbury, Kent CT2 7BD
Review by Eileen Elias

"The Past is our Looking Glass" is a fitting title to the first chapter of Gloria Jarvis Smith's absorbing book of family history. Gloria traces her direct ancestors, right back to "The Last Will and Testament of Richard Jervis, Husbandman of Haddenham, written in 1557 - the Catholic England of Mary Tudor" she has obviously enjoyed the search.

The book has a special interest for me since the Genealogical Society gave me my first job on leaving college long ago. The book concludes with notes on a distant ancestor, William de Carun, shown in 'Domesday' as a knight owning land in Bedfordshire. I recommend it for anyone interested in history.

The Woman Writer June 2004

A Jarvis Tapestry, Part II.
by Gloria Jarvis Smith. Illustrations by Gloria and Rupert V Jarvis. Published by the author, The Bungalow, Tyler Close, Canterbury, Kent CT2 7BD.
Price £5.99 + £2 pp.
Review by Peggy Crossland

This second volume of the history of the Jarvis family succeeds in maintaining the same high standard as the first. Not only is it well written and carefully researched, it is also lavishly illustrated.

Any reader who imagines that history is as dry as dust would do well to read it as it illuminates the past in an irresistable way. The years from the Twenties through to modern times are covered in this book. For those of us of a certain age it is not just nostalgia which makes us long for the lives and experiences of ordinary people to be recorded with such sympathetic understanding. This is an important piece of social history.

For the historical novelist it is a feast of delights with inspiration for a book on every page. A strong creative streak has blessed these talented writers, actors, painters and musicians throughout the years. The spirit of adventure is not missing either, leading them to search beyond these shores for partners, a long way from that original Tudor yeoman, Richard of Haddenham in Buckinghamshire.

This is a great book for dipping into. Presently, my favourite bedtime reading.

The Woman Writer June 2004

A JARVIS TAPESTRY – PART II
Gloria Jarvis Smith, 0095365615
This book continues the fascinating story of the author's family history from Edwardian times to the present day. (The first volume was reviewed in issue 25; August 2003 of the Review) With photographs and Gloria's own delightful sketches, this book interweaves the story of a family with the social backdrop of their times. Those wishing to research life in the home counties in the early 20th century will find this book invaluable.

Both books can be bought from Gloria Jarvis Smith, The Bungalow, Tyler Close, Canterbury, Kent CT2 7BC for £5.99 each plus £2 each p&p.
Sally Zigmond

THE HISTORICAL NOVELS REVIEW

ISSUE 28, MAY 2004

A Jarvis Tapestry Parts I and II

A Jarvis Tapestry by Gloria Jarvis Smith is the early history of a Buckinghamshire family from Tudor to Victorian times. *A Jarvis Tapestry Part II* continues the story of an Edwardian family of Aylesbury at home through the 1920s and 1930s to modern times. Both books are well illustrated with photographs, drawings and family trees and are £5.99 each, plus £2 postage and packing (UK). They can be obtained from Gloria Jarvis Smith at 38 St Radigund Street, Canterbury, Kent CT1 2AA.

september 2004 family tree magazine

Book Reviews

APPENDICES

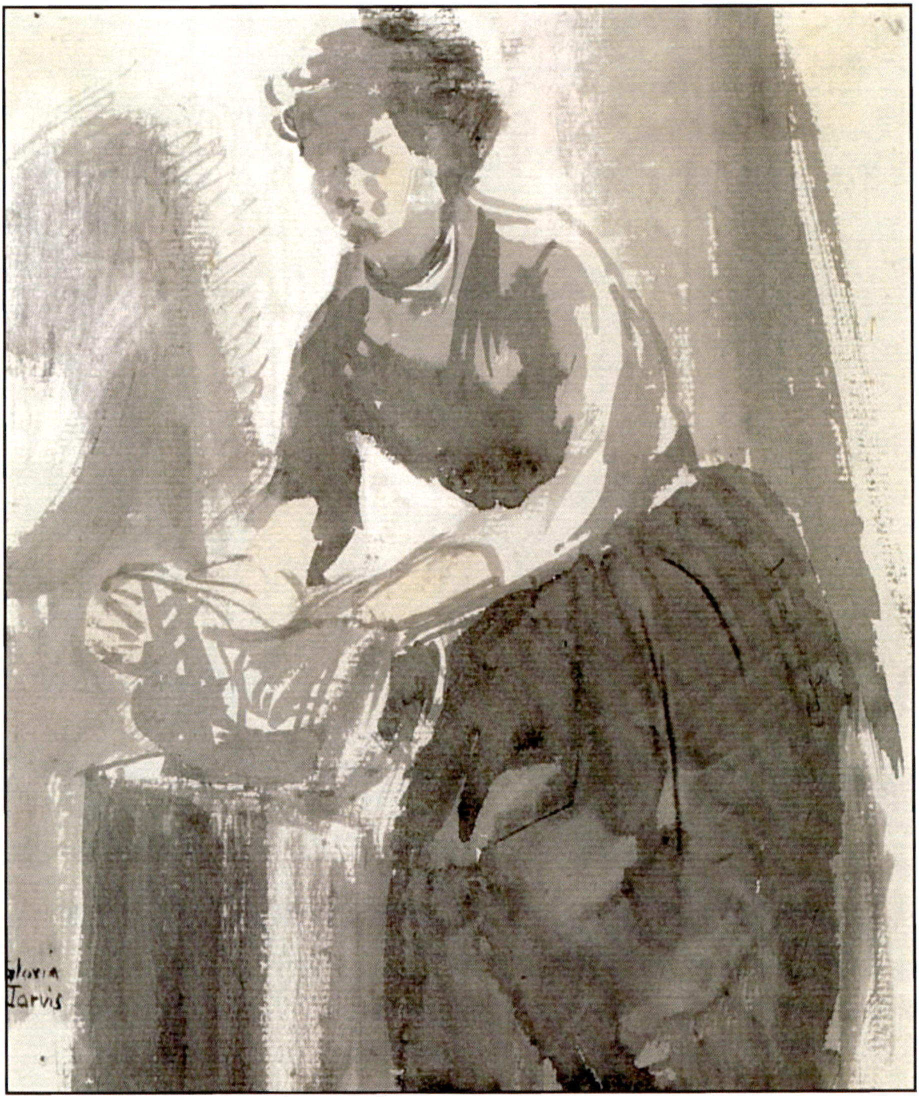
Gloria
Jarvis

GLORIA JARVIS SMITH – A Lady of many talents

By Margaret Crosland

Gloria Jarvis Smith is writing a family history which may provide the answer to an intriguing question. Just how large a part is played by heredity in the creation of a person who is not only a gifted artist, but also a poet, playwright, author and journalist? Gloria's maternal forebears were Italian. Her grandfather came from Emilia – a craftsman who worked with the great Malatesta upon the mosaics in Westminster Cathedral. Her English father was a well-known graphics artist and illustrator. Spurred on by his example Gloria trained at St Martin's School of Art in London and later at the University of Florence. She graduated with honours and later became a lecturer on historic costume and an instructor in costume drawing at the Polytechnic in Regent Street.

As a teenager she had also enjoyed writing, but it was when she married and moved to Brussels with her husband that the editor of the Brussels Times asked her for some pieces with a British flavour.

A successful painter by that time she had already won the Medaille d'Argent in Paris and the Italian Medaille d'Or. Much of her work was in permanent collections in Belgium in oils, water-colour, pastel, ink and gouache. Her portrait of Princess Paola of Liège had captured all the sweetness of her young subject, and a painting of Margaret Thatcher was said to be a favourite with that lady's husband.

Even so, the opportunity to work in another creative field was too good to miss. Gloria began to write short pieces for the Brussels Times and The Beacon (British Community News). She started with art and theatre reviews and reports on events of Belgo-British interest. Markets in Brussels and Walks in Brussels followed and tongue-in-cheek, A Look at Local Loos.

This was a surprising choice of subject for the resident painter at 'Old England' – a department store as exclusive as Fortnum and Mason, and an artist whose painting of a Frost Fair on the Thames had been exhibited at the Royal Academy and now hung beside a Rubens in the proud owner's private collection, but Gloria is a surprising person.

Quiet-voiced and modest she has a wicked sense of humour, sharp powers of observation, and a sparkling wit reserved for the most part for the enjoyment of her closest friends.

Encouraged by the success of her early writing she went on to produce short stories which were broadcast on BBC Radio 4 and the World Service. Her work also appeared in the annual exhibitions of manuscripts of l'Association Royal des Ecrivains Wallons. She then became a member of the Union Mondiale de la Presse Feminine.
On her return to England, Gloria settled in Canterbury. She was still painting, but a change of eyesight in middle age caused difficulties. She turned more and more to writing.

In 1990 she joined the SWWJ. Then she became Chairman of Canterbury Writers' Group, taking part in their annual performances of original poetry and prose at the Canterbury Festival. One of her poems, Rose in the Martydom appeared in a Tributes in Verse anthology published in Poetry Now. For four years in succession her work was read at the London Drama Festival held at the Goodrich Theatre in Putney.
Gloria's interest in history has never flagged and a project dear to her heart is to act as guide at Canterbury Cathedral, where she makes full use of her fluent French and Italian when showing groups of foreign tourists round the historic site.

The BBC has accepted one of her plays for radio, but at present the family history is her major concern. In years to come this carefully researched work may prove invaluable to social historians. It traces the life of a family of English yeomen back to mediaeval times on her father's side. The exotic flavour of Italian blood adds mystery to the story.

Many of us would like to trace our ancestry, yet few of us have the patience to search through ancient documents, picking up snippets of information from wills and parish registers. Gloria has done so, and the book, when finished, should provide a fascinating insight into the making of a writer.

From "The Woman Writer" -
journal of The Society of Women Writers and Journalists

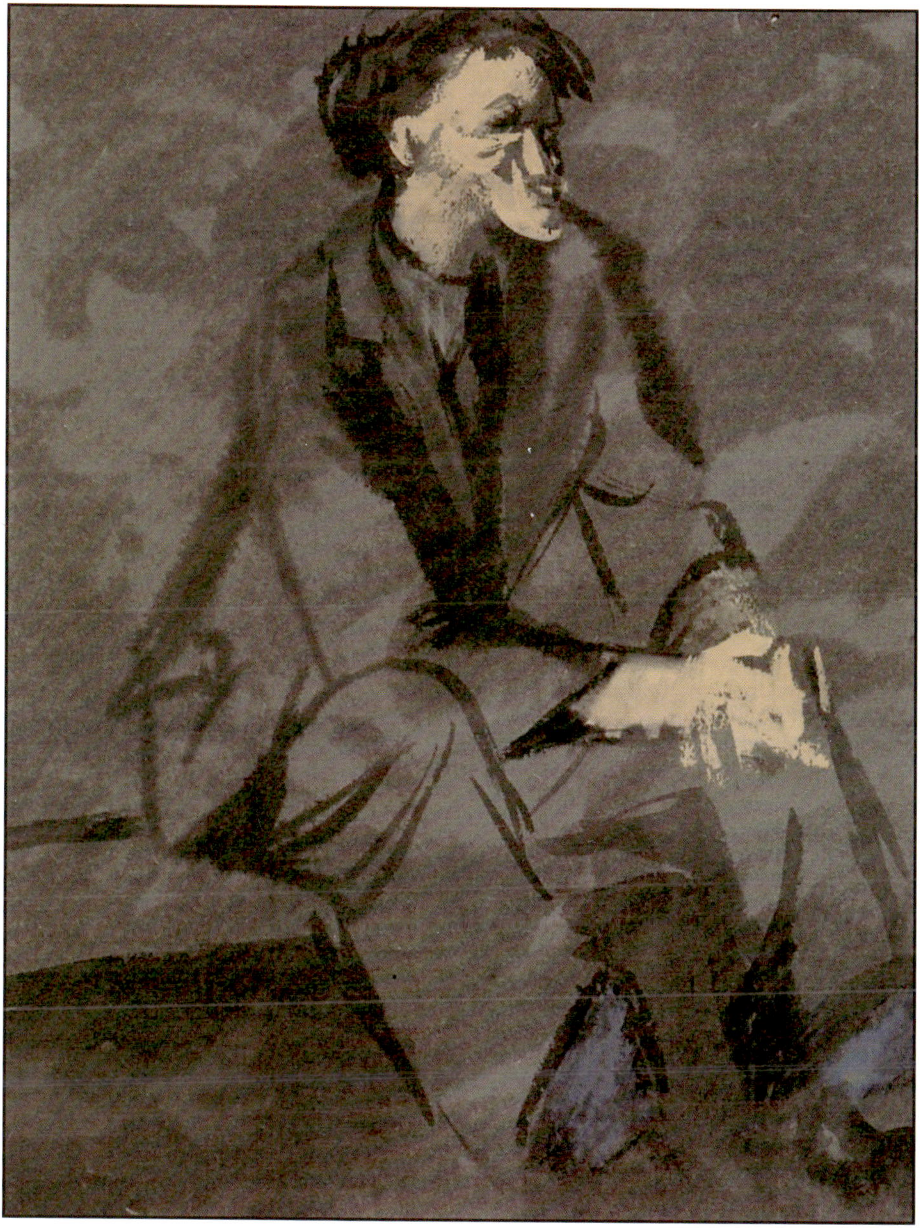

Christiane Schietecatte

a le plaisir de vous inviter au salon d'ensemble

heeft het genoegen U uit te nodigen op de gezamenlijke tentoonstelling

Les Chemins du Coeur

Avec des œuvres choisies de :

Met uitgelezen werken van :

ABEL - CARON - ANTO CARTE - BAIJOT
Jacques CHAIDRON - Charles COUNHAYE - Charles DE COORDE - A. de la BARRE
René DAUBIES - Frans DEPOOTER - Jean-Jacques GAILLIARD - Willy GILBERT
A.J. HEYMANS - HOLMEAD - Georgina ISERBYT - Gloria JARVIS
Sylvain LAMBRE - Georges LEMMEN - Marcel LUCAS - Paul MAAS
Medard MAERTENS - Marc MONKOWICKI - Marcel MORTIER
Claudine NEMIROVSKY - Willem PAERELS -Albert PINOT - Alfred ROZELAAR-GREEN - SCHIRREN - Harry SLEIJSER - Marcel STOBBAERTS
Rodolph STREBELLE - Charles SWYNCOP - Pierre THEVENET - Lidia VAJDA
Jean VAN WEL - VAN ZEVENBERGHEN - VERAG - Médard VERBURGH
Taf WALLET - Fernand WERY - Ferdinand WILLAERT
Maggy WILLEMSEN - WOLVENS

Cocktail 19/8/82 *à / te* *19* *h. / u.*

HORIZONS

Gloria Jarvis - gouaches et pastels

expose à **l'Astelle**

Cocktail : jeudi 8 décembre de 18 à 21 heures.
Exposition : du 9 au 31 décembre.

Passage Linthout, 11 - 14 – 1040 Bruxelles – Tél. 734.20.84
Ouvert de 10 h. à 19 h. Sauf le dimanche et le lundi matin.

Two of the many galleries where I exhibited

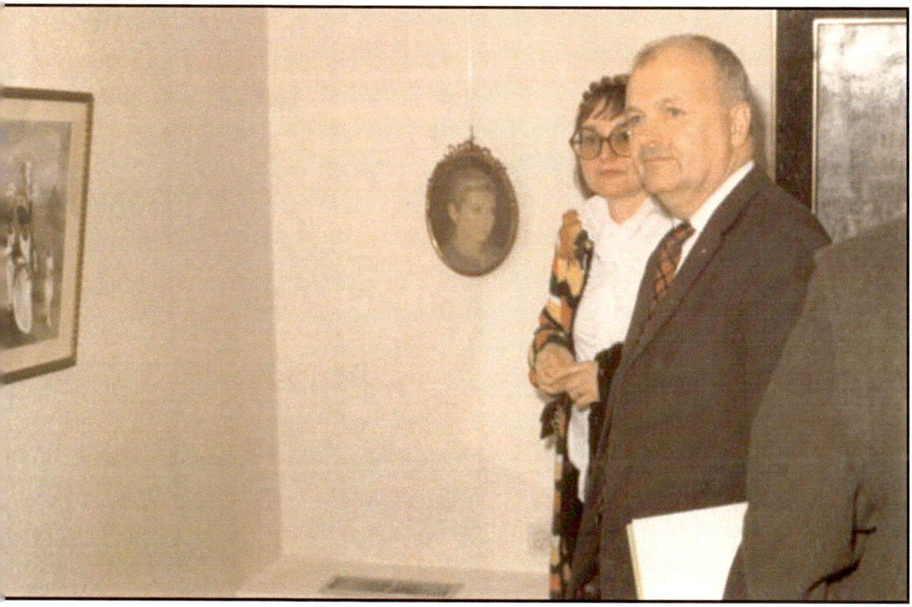

I accompany the Bourgemestre at one of my exhibitions at the Centre Culturelle Beco.

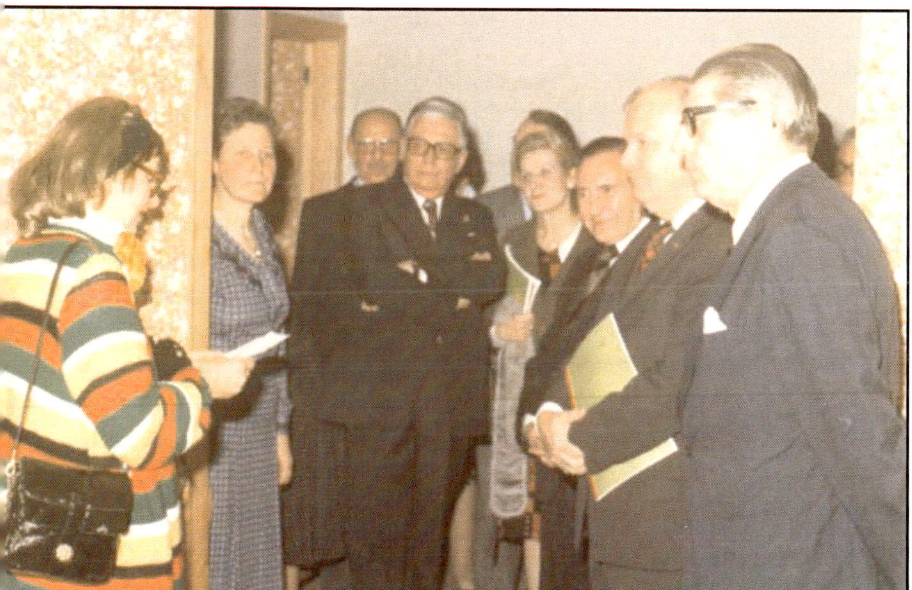

I address the worthies of the Commune at the opening of one of my exhibitions.